AGILE, HELP ME OUT

Journey of Agile Practices. Honoring Past.

A S LEO SCORPIONIES,
NANDHINI V,
SUMA R,
RAMYA K,
BHRAMINI NTR

Preface

Being a martial arts lover, I always admired the skills of martial arts fighters who can defend with ease and quick. The techniques of martial arts enable the warrior in developing war skills. Such warriors have protected the nation from time to time. They are capable and can face any uncertainties in wars with ease.

Like any martial arts warriors, project team requires to face many challenges to be agile. One must understand the evolution of these agile process, methods and frameworks. We must understand the specific purpose of practices to get the desired benefits in our work.

This book is an attempt to sneak into agile history and methods followed in past and bring it together. These flexible and easy methods in different phases of developments enable team agility.

Hope you enjoy reading and gain good knowledge. We look forward to your valuable comments and improvements.

- *A S Leo Scorpionies*

Preface

Agile practices in today projects are key to success of delivery. As agile coach, experience in training teams on agile practices has been more beneficial and value driven based on right set of games played during training programs.

As frameworks being classified as Domain and lifecycle frameworks. These frameworks are adopted in organization and methods are defined for team to follow standard process to get best delivery from teams.

Considering Martial arts background, the domain frameworks are closer to weapons type and lifecycle frameworks are towards strategy adopted. The methodology improves team skills based on standard process and methods towards facing project challenges and considered as guiding book.

Few games have been identified from world of athletics and creative sports, closer to agile practices.

- *Nandhini V, Ramya K , Suma R, Bhramini NTR*

Contents

PART A

Agile Journey

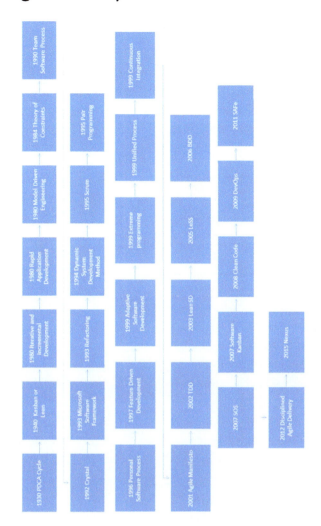

Frameworks at Glance

Agile Framework Types	Description
1980 MDE	Model Driven Engineering promotes design using models or visual diagrams over detailed specification
1984 TOC	Theory of Constraints focus finds constraints on the connected process around the system. It adopts idiom "Chain is no stronger than its weakest link".
1990 TSP	Team software process recommends methods to organize projects and building team. It supports methods to measure and derive metrics to improve the software process.
1992 Crystal	Developing software by focusing on people, interactions, skills, talents, communication and community. It is a people-centric framework and prescribes a wider range of roles.
1993 MSF	Microsoft Software Framework (MSF) is a set of principles, models, methods and guidelines. It is the first comprehensive framework covering the complete development life cycle. MSF adopts Project management, CMMI, Agile and Risks methods and process.
1993 Refactoring	Refactoring insists improvements on long and duplicate codes. Advocates to rewrite without impacting functionality. It promotes maintainability and extendibility in product development as key aspects.
1994 DSDM	Dynamic System Development Methods is a development life cycle framework. It embraces Rapid Application Development processes and methods to its core.

1995 Scrum		Scrum is a lightweight framework based timebox called sprints. It recommends small teams, few roles and simple methods to manage the team.
1996 PSP		Personal Software Process recommends a disciplined personal framework to perform software work.
1997 FDD		Feature Driven Development promotes software development around requirements features.
1999 ASD		Adaptive Software Development is a direct outgrowth of an earlier Rapid Application Development.
1999 XP		Extreme Programming is a Code first approach to software development. It emphasizes four basic activities: coding, testing, listening, and designing.
1999 UP		Unified Process is an iterative and incremental software development process framework
1999 CI		Continuous Integration insists on code integrity and readiness.
2001 AM		The Agile Manifesto is a proclamation that articulates four key values and 12 principles.
2002 TDD		Test-driven development is a software development process recommending the fail first approach. At first, the developer writes a failing test case and then code to pass that test.
2003 LSD		Lean software development is a translation of lean manufacturing principles and practices to the software development domain
2005 LeSS		Large-Scale Scrum (LeSS) is a framework for scaled agile and scaling Scrum. LeSS decreases organizational complexity.

2006 BDD	Behavior Driven Development is a software engineering process that stems from Test Driven Development (TDD) and Acceptance Test-Driven Development (ATDD).
2007 SOS	Scrum of Scrums is a scaled agile technique for extending scrum to many teams.
2007 SK	Software Kanban is a method for managing the creation of products with an emphasis on continual delivery while not overburdening the development team.
2008 CC	Clean Code is a guideline provided to help developers to write better and cleaner code.
2009 DevOps	DevOps is a software development practices combining software development and technology operations. Its focus is to reduce the timeline in delivering updates, features and fixes
2011 SAFe	The Scaled Agile Framework guides enterprises to follow agile practices at large scale
2012 DAD	Disciplined Agile Delivery is a people-first and learning-oriented approach to IT solution delivery. It embraces a goal-driven approach and is scalable.
2015	Nexus is a framework that drives in minimizing cross-team dependencies and integration issues.
Yet to Publish	VISA Methodology in development and expected date of release in FY 2020.

Values & Principles

Agile Values

1. Individuals and Interactions Over Processes and Tools

If the process or the tools causes the team to be less responsive to change then they can override such a process. Interactions and collaboration are more important over the process.

2. Working Software Over Comprehensive Documentation

Agile encourages the developer to adopt visual practices over comprehensive-textual documentation. It recommends diagrams to give enough information and clarity instead of long documents.

The practice helps the agile team to be much faster in producing relevant documents. The Agile Manifesto values documentation, but it values working software more.

3. Customer Collaboration Over Contract Negotiation

Negotiation is the period when customer and Service provider work out on alternatives. Many times, cost, time and scope drive alternatives. These may compromise and limit benefits. It could even lead to the product getting shelved much earlier than expected.

Agile values on customer collaboration and frequent interaction towards building the right products. This collaboration improves customer involvement and evolution at their own pace and budget. It derives value adds to business based on priority and needs of customer than on budget aspects.

4. Responding to Change Over Following a Plan

Many times, due to regulatory and business needs, the earlier requirements need updates. The plans may no longer meet end goals and need change. Accommodating changes are important to business than following a plan with no values.

Principles of Agile

1. Our highest priority is to satisfy the customer through early and continuous delivery of valuable software.
2. Welcome changing requirements, even late in development. Agile processes harness change for the customer's competitive advantage.
3. Deliver working software frequently, from a couple of weeks to a couple of months, with a preference to the shorter timescale.
4. Business people and developers must work together daily throughout the project.
5. Build projects around motivated individuals. Give them the environment and support they need and trust them to get the job done.
6. The most efficient and effective method of conveying information to and within a development team is face-to-face conversation.
7. Working software is the primary measure of progress.
8. Agile processes promote sustainable development. The sponsors, developers, and users should be able to maintain a constant pace indefinitely.
9. Continuous attention to technical excellence and good design enhances agility.
10. Simplicity—the art of maximizing the amount of work not done—is essential.
11. The best architectures, requirements, and designs emerge from self-organizing teams.
12. At regular intervals, the team reflects on how to become more effective, then tunes and adjusts its behaviour accordingly.

Agile Team

Agile is moving faster or quicker with ease. The team needs to move faster with ease and adopt practices enabling agility. The quick team is capable of accommodating changes.

The Scrum framework recommend an agile team with 3 roles.

The Scrum formation of the team became a standard approach for agile projects. The scrum limited team to be between 5-9 members and adopt 2- 4-week sprints.

Timebox and team size promote interaction and collaboration within the team.

Team Size: The size of the team is between 5-9 members.

Team formation: The team must consist of essential members required to deliver the product.

Team Roles: Below are 3 team roles agile team follows.

Product Owner

The product owner is one who provides inputs to the team on the product scope and objectives. Product owner owns product backlogs. The backlogs consist of user stories and associated priority. These are further grouped by features and belongs to an epic.

Scrum Master

Scrum Master is one who coordinates with team and practices agile ceremonies. He is responsible to ensure the team delivers agreed commitments for each sprint.

He practices stand-up meetings between 10-15 minutes daily to unblock impediments. He ensures effective collaboration and improvements by organizing sprint review and retrospective meetings. Along with product owner tracks the progress of team measuring velocity and burndowns.

Team Members

The team is responsible to deliver functionalities committed at the end of each sprint. They take part in all ceremonies and work towards functional products. Agile Team must be collaborative, self-organizing and focused in sprint goal and delivery. They work together to deliver either a shippable or workable product.

Agile Team Practices

Backlog Planning

User-story: It is a description of user actions on application towards meeting expected result.

Feature: user-stories grouped on specific services or functionality.

Epic: Journey of user experience in availing product services. It consists of features and user stories.

Backlog Refinement

Refinement is a review process validating and elaborating details of the user story. Acceptance criteria are detailed and agreed within the team.

Backlog Grooming

Grooming is an important communication and collaboration process to explain user stories to the team.

Backlog Estimates

Once grooming is done, Estimation kick-offs. The team determines the complexity and effort required for backlog items.

Sprint Planning

Once estimated, the Number of sprints or iterations is determined to complete the product. The number of sprints is computed based on velocity or capacity. Then work items are allocated to each sprint based on the order of priority.

Sprint Board

Represents work items movement from one stage to another in table format.

Sprint review

Sprint review focuses and ensures work items consist of enough details and acceptance criteria to work.

Any customer changes on completed functionalities may include in the upcoming sprint. At the sprint review stage, all details must present with acceptance criteria. The team can either accept or reject work-item on doable.

Sprint review revisits upcoming sprints to complete backlog items. New sprints can also get added. It's important to determine impact before descoping work items from the backlog.

Stand-up meeting

A short meeting to know impediments of the team.

Showcase

The showcase is an opportunity to show off the great work, the team have been doing and get feedback from the product owner or end customer.

Sprint Retrospective

It helps the team to connect and communicate on things that can be improved in upcoming sprints to meet product goals. It also helps in deciding key strategies and approach for the project or product environment.

Velocity measurement

It is a crucial metric that determines team ability to deliver work items and impact towards product delivery schedule.

Burndown

The work completed and remaining against allocated in graphical format.

PART B

Let's Begin Agility

- First things First
- Agility in Requirements
- Agility in Design
- Agility in Code
- Agility in Testing
- Agility in Support

First things First

Before team starts its development, they must have answers to few questions as listed.

Roadmap
      What are you here for?
      What are you building or supporting?
      What does application do?
Expectation
      What is expected and when it is expected?
      Who is going to sign-off?
      Who owns requirements?
      Who is responsible for requirements?
      What technology is being used?
      What artifacts would be provided?
Environment
      Are development and Test environments Ready?
      Are environments consistent or different?
Constraints
      Does team have skills required?
      Do I need to train team?
      Is schedule and budget fixed for identified scope?
      Do we have any dependencies with external parties?
Risks
      Are requirements complete?
      Will requirements evolve?
      Any dependencies with external vendors?
Process
      What development and team processes are agreed?
      Does team know delivery process?
      Does team understand agree on processes?
      How does team collaborate and interact?
      How does team ensure to be on same page across cross functional skill team?
Tools
      What is team management tool?
      What tool does BA uses?
      What are TA tools?
      What is Dev and Test Tools?
Roles
      What is my team responsibility?
      What does my team do if they got blocked?
      What artifacts they are responsible for?
Alignment & Agreement
      Are team members clear with product backlog and sprint scope?
      Do team members know where QA sign off is done?

Are team clear on roles and responsibilities?

Does team understand escalation channel and stakeholders' priorities?

Does team understand on review and clarifications process?

Requirements

Have team members got enough details required to develop and test user story?

What is permissible rework% or estimation% variance for team?

Does team follow As-Is basis model?

Does team follow prototype or interactive or value driven model?

How is quality measured?

NFRs

Are NFRs clear to team?

Infrastructure

Are they able to perform test run on identified environments using defined development process and tools?

Compliances

Is team clear on mandatory compliance from project governance – timesheet, attendance, leave plans, etc.

Strategy and Approach

Is team cleared on team strategy, approach, process and tools being used in team?

Team Readiness

Are there any constraints and dependencies on environments & tools?

Every team member must aware <u>ecosystem and goals</u>.

Agility in Requirements

Requirements are primary input to team. It is very important for team to have clear understanding of requirements and enough details to proceed with development to deliver shippable and workable product.

A shippable product is not workable or complete product, rather any functionalities of complete product that customer can view and use. - tangible results.

Requirements volatility or stability is key for team to decide on team development strategy towards meeting product goals and delivery.

If requirements are stable, then team is all set to GO.

On other hand, if requirements are instable then it's time to take backstep and identify strategy to finalize on approach before moving forward.

This would help team to achieve sprint goals, customer satisfaction, customer collaboration and team agility to meet project goals.

Before we start further, let's look at some common practices considered in agile world for requirements.

All requirements must be clear and complete. It should ideally follow INVEST model (Independent, Negotiable, Valuable, Estimable, Small, Testable).
FDD and BDD Agile framework details methods and practices to ensure quality of user stories. It's worth looking into these practices and follow them to gain agility within the team.

In general practice, ensure you have performed below steps before you move to Design.

- User Stories as requirements.
- User stories must follow INVEST model.
- Group by functionality.
- Group by Epic or User Journey(flow).
- Identify critical and not critical flows.
- User journey is our goal (end to end flow), not user page interactions.
- Focus on scenarios and behaviors.
- Model scenarios and behaviors.

<u>User stories as requirements</u>

Ensure best practice in defining user story in form of User-Action-Result.

> As a <type of users / Persona>, I want to <goal>, so that <result>

User stories must follow INVEST model

Follow INVEST Model (Independent, Negotiable, Valuable, Estimable, Small, Testable).

Independent – Can be developed and tested without any impact to other functionalities

Negotiable – ability to break the functionalities to smaller independent units

Valuable – must be of customer or business values, tangible output of business acceptances.

Estimable – must be able to determine effort and complexity

Small – Must be able to complete development (build and test) within sprint.

Testable – must be able to verify and validate the interaction against scenario independently

Group by functionality.

Group user stories to functional area, usually called as "Feature".

EPIC – As a valid application user, I want to select and add products, so that I can perform payment and order now or later.

Feature: Shopping cart
- Browse items
- View items by category
- Compare items
- Add to shopping cart
- View shopping cart items
- Remove items from shopping cart
- View itemized and total cost
- Preserve shopping cart for later additions.

Feature: Payment
- Pay by card
- Cash on delivery
- Pay on delivery
- Pay by bank
- Equated Monthly installment

Feature: Cancellation and Refund
- View confirmed orders
- Cancel confirmed orders
- Refund by account

Group by Epic or User journey (flow)

Group features by Epic. Epic is flow of actions performed to complete the service request by user or representative.

Example: In e-commerce application user must be able to perform online payment for items selected in cart and get confirmation and dispatch details.

The above is a user journey to checkout items. However, to complete above user journey, the user will interact and perform multiple steps. These steps are related and could belong to other features or functionality.

Example:

The journey could consist of below functionalities or features to complete above user journey or epic.

1) Signup
2) Listing and searching catalog
3) Cart Management – Add, Delete, Modify
4) Checkout – Payment and order confirmation
5) Confirmation – Payment confirmation and dispatch or order status.
6) Notification – Order status.

And each of these features consists set of user story and interactions (behaviors) to complete functionality and move on to next step to complete journey to obtain service.

As a team, we must be clear on above journeys (epics) and process involved. These are represented in form of swim lane, story board, persona (role).

Many times, the above epics and connected processes are only ones available to team in form of high-level requirements. The customer may not have finalized on look and feel of each page associated to features or user story.

And Team, must not be inclined towards minute details to start design and development. The application must not be dependent on page level details, rather on process of business service flow.

EPIC (user journey) – As a valid application user, I want to select and add products, so that I can perform payment and order now or later.

- Epic: User Journey or business Service (system)
- Journey story board (visual flow (functional flow & process flow)
  - Feature: domain functionality (sub-system)
    - Functional User story / Scenarios
    - Functional Storyboard (form or page flow & process flow)
      - Page interaction or behaviors (conditional scenarios) against functional scenarios.

The Design team can come up with low-fidelity wireframes for more clarity towards attributes or parameters required of process associated with page flows or process flow.

The requirements team usually are more focused towards look and feel needs of customer and wireframes produced consists these granular details. These are referred as high-fidelity wireframes.

However, wireframes are rough sketch, the mockup is created by development team either by UX developer or web developer. These mockup helps design and development team to know how the product would look at end for customer (these details are not blocker for development team and could develop much later once they are available)

Identify critical and non-critical flows.

Development team must give more importance to application flows or epics and features rather than look and feel.

Adding, Complete product called as working product is made up of critical and non-critical flows (collection of user stories).

For example; In shopping cart example, there could be functionality to change password based on security policy. If the above functionality is not working, it may not impact the core service of checkout and impact is very minimal. Such flow could be treated as non-critical flow not impacting core service.

User journey is our goal (end to end / Epic).

The goal of development team is to deliver the product to perform user actions on journey or epic.

It is important for development team to have clear information to avoid rework or changes to design.

However, development team must always consider second priority to look and feel of product and focus more on actions and dependencies against epic, features and interaction.

At times, the requirements team may not have details or waiting for details from customer on look and feel to develop mock-up.

The look and feel may get impacted, but not action flow of product. It is good to refine look and feel later sprints rather than stressing on them upfront.

In scenarios, where explicit or customer standards and expectation are inclined towards look and feel, then it is good to ensure we have high-fidelity wireframes, story-boards, mock-ups.

Sketch

Wireframe

Mockup

The above would help team to quickly build prototype to showcase to customer for further elicitation or elaboration towards final workable product goals.

It is very important, when look and feel is equally important as part of shippable or workable product, team does have those details.

The team must look/ask for wireframes, mockups, data validation, error validation and other NFRs required.

It is good to have visuals, rather than textual descriptions in form sentences or paragraphs.

Focus on scenarios and behaviors

EPIC (user journey) – As a valid application user, I want to select and add products, so that I can perform payment and order now or later.

- Epic: User Journey or business Service (system)
- Journey story board (visual flow (functional flow & process flow)
  - Feature: domain functionality (sub-system)
    - Functional User story / Scenarios
    - Functional Storyboard (form or page flow & process flow)
      - Page interaction or behaviors (conditional scenarios) against functional scenarios.

As insisted, the development team must give importance to scenarios and behaviors of product being developed.

The scenarios and behaviors are contractual agreement for both developers and testers towards sign-off for product flows.

It also helps both developers and testers to develop test cases and map it against scenarios and behaviors.

It is good to consider each user interaction as scenarios and different conditions to behaviors. It is important to also consider the scenarios may be limited to functionality or feature only. Such reduced scope may not help development team much when scope is more towards user journey.

Hence, the team must ensure all related scenarios and behaviors are grouped and mapped for better quality.

The FDD and BDD framework does not insists testers to adopt to follow practices for better agility.

<u>Model scenarios and behaviors.</u>

Navigation Flow Diagram represents user journey and interaction. Navigation flow diagram help team to understand primary and alternative flows of system. This information helps architects and developer to adopt better design patterns and solutions.

The story board is another format to describe on product functionality based on user journeys.

The story-board can evolve over period from concept model to prototype depending on context.

In case, if team is not clear with requirements and conflicts between team members. It is good to come up with conceptual flow and agree on it with team and customer or product owner.

The team can further request for rich formats of story-board to determine on additional effort required for final workable product to customer.

The below picture shares idea on how conceptual evolves to prototype in team. The richer ones are developed by Business Analyst or User Interface developer or by development team.

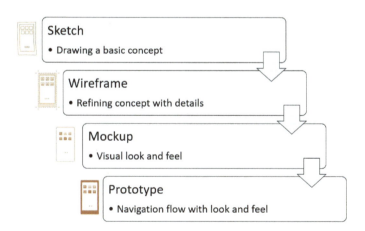

As a Team, it is important to avoid minute details in agile development. The focus must be on flow, process and actions. Look and feel to be last priority towards delivering shippable and workable product. Such practices enable agile team towards successful development and delivery.

Agility in Design

Agile Design is very important. Technology Architect or design team must honor and avoid detailed textual specification. The focus to be on models and diagrams for better agility within team.

Design Developers should be aware of industry best practices in design modelling and be comfortable to implement.

Make sure as Design developer you produce application architectures, component interactions diagrams, user case diagrams, activity flow diagrams, sequence diagrams, data flow and entity relationship.

It is important for agile team to focus on Just in time design and development based on information available. They need to follow Joint Application Development sessions and focus on workable product.

Design changes due to evolving requirements in agile world. Just in Time and refactoring ensures team agility and avoid reworks.

Many agile design developers are under impression that agile is more towards team process and practices and not related to design and development.

To obtain agility in team, the team must follow and adhere to agile practices across phases to get overall agile benefits.
Ensure all team members are fully aware of product flows and related design artifacts. Such approach helps all team members in evaluating impact on system due to changes.

We have gamut of design models or diagrams, but ensure you keep it to minimum. In Agile team, these models can be refactored iteratively, and incrementally developed as new requirements or changes comes to the team.

Application Architecture – Application architecture provides information on application layers and major component interaction within system or product.

Use case – Use case are diagrams depicting the actor's interaction with system. It gives insights to developers on actors and system components collaborations.

It is first diagram design developer or development team would look to understand how application interacts with its components. These components are related to features of product.

Component interaction diagram is very crucial to development team when many developers are involved in developing product.

The model helps developers to logically understand interaction between them and trace easily during hotfixes.

Activity Diagram
It gives enough details for developers to look at primary and alternative flows of user actions. It enables developers to handle exception and validation for given scenario.

Sequence Diagram
If activity diagrams provide information on primary and alternative flow for given scenario. The sequence diagrams enrich activity diagram by providing sub-components interaction and method calls to fulfill objectives of scenario towards expected outcome over a period. The diagram removes confusion of developers on dependency and relationship within components and sub-components.

Data Flow – The is important for developers and tester to understand how data flows within system. This information is required for developers to model components, identify inheritance, association with other sub-components or classes.

Entity relationship: This diagram provides required insights to developers on application database and refinements.

As we conclude, it is important to note, the above are recommendation for agile team to keep the design specification short and simple. At same time ensuring required information are available to development team and other supporting teams.

Please keep in mind, as requirements evolve, design and code refactor is must to accommodate new changes. The iterative and incremental practices help design developers to design based on requirements available and be open to changes for requirements inflight.

Agility in Code

Developers are required to be flexible and quick to implement changes to the codes.

In agile team, the developers experience, and practices followed influence team agility towards successful development.

Frameworks like TDD, retrospective, refactoring and clean code helps developer to be more agile. They gamut of architectures and principles helping developers to be agile at best.

SOLID principles, Interface driven, Mockup and domain driven practices helps developers to focus Just in Time design and development by adopting patterns and practices to meet end-2-flow.

The development team must come out of mindset of one-time coding based on availability of detail design. In agile world developers need to focus on iterative and incremental approaches and be agile by adopting Just in time and JAD session to write and build codes.

The skills of developers are very crucial in agile team due to nature of requirements volatility, design and code evolution. Refactoring skills are must and be daily practices and adopting parallel development approaches increase agile and agility in meeting deliverables on time.

It is always required all agile team members are focused towards user interactions and flow and developers must focus based on team strategy adopted for coding and unit testing, it could be mockup or prototype based on interface and stub model using tools like SOAP UI.

Many projects get into parallel development mode due to external API dependencies either in development or undergoes changes impacting core product. This must be minimized by ensuring these interfaces are prone to change and trust factors must be kept at low.

In agile, since focus is more towards shippable product from user perspective, the flow or behavior represented in form of user stories and test conditions enables developers to be more focused on user journey as highest priority.

It forces developers to identify flow and classes at abstract level with stubs and mockups. Since application frameworks and functional components can evolve sprint after sprint, it is very important to adopt practices that gives agility to team.

As TDD enforces follow fail first approach to get flow ready before moving to page level data and error validation.

As repeated and insisted, End-2-End flow is very important for developers, it is good to get all layer components at abstract level by using stub or mock-up end-2-end and performing unit test before moving out to next level.

Typically, the developers would be focusing from UI layer to Component layer to API layer to Data Layer. To ensure refactoring and flexible design to be adopted incremental, it is good to focus from end user rather domain focused or sub-system focused.

The domain and sub-system focus may not only derail the project timeline, it could result in late involvement with customer and product owners and results in effort and schedule overrun.

Hence, we need to focus in moving from one layer to another with speed by adopting mockup and stub before moving towards concrete implementation of functions or methods within code. This approach helps us to revisit and refactor our code with all developers and add more value to our joint session and product or shippable product development incrementally.

It is recommended to adopt interface driven practices to segregate stub or mockup with core implementation with help of product or project interfaces benefiting unit test and to gain knowledge towards right development against user stories focused towards end-2end. Interface based approach helps to keep mockup and stub separate without impacting our core implementation or integration with external API and minimize out application failover due to changes at later point in time.

Follow SOLID principles, this really helps for agile developers due to it benefits in keeping code simple and less complicated and focused on single responsibility and helping to refactor as greater speed complementing requirements volatility or changing needs.

At time, the agile developers might involve and own database components from tables, view and store procedures based on conceptual models that are evolving sprint after sprint.

It is good for developers to create such component just in time and refactor as sprint focus based on user story picked by team.

In agile team, normalization and denormalization is continuous activity and development team must be agile and be aware of such changes. It is important for team to involve in JAD and team session to ensure they are aligned and aware of evolution or progressive changes.

As earlier pointed, do not worry about design issues or normalization; Ensure you do refactor as you move from one flow to another flow in alignment to BDD/FDD recommendations. This helps your design evolve over period.

Ensure every time you add new tables or write new code you follow design guidelines, relook what is available, Can I **reuse** existing one or extended new ones, do I need to normalize or de-normalize based on new changes?

Please note, you need to refactor and ensure previous flows do not get any impact; It is important to note all layers would or might get into refactoring zone. This must be considered as part of user story complexity and effort must be factored as journey moves on in agile team.

To conclude, developers are recommended to adopt iterative and incremental design and coding approaches rather than first time right approach to ensure better agility, productivity towards deliverables meeting customer expectation or product functionalities.

Agility in Test

As we all know testing is based on verification and validation, in first we are ensuring team is performing right steps. In second, we are ensuring team has delivered what is expected as per given requirements.

The Testing in Agile starts in very early stages and embraces V-Model, FDD and BDD in agile teams.
It is required, requirements need to be reviewed and verified to ensure it meets customer needs.

During Inception stages it is best to adopt FDD and V-Model to ensure we adopt best of both world in identifying functional requirements based on domain or functionalities of product and perform parallel review and verification process

Once moved out of inception stage after obtaining clarity on broad functionalities and expected behavior, we need to move to next best practice – BDD. This process helps in complementing or elaborating more towards user interaction or action in system. It is aligning towards storyboard and user journey.

When your user stories follow FDD and INVEST recommendation, your user story representing Action-Goal-Result acts as scenarios representing end to end flow of product from user perspective against functional domain, cutting across more than functional domain or other product features.

In such scenarios, BDD recommendation best helps the testing team to adopt and write test condition to measure product quality from user behavior and expectation, helping overall quality of product. It also helps in segregation or grouping of test condition to Negative, Positive, Boundary, Security, Responsive, Accessibility, failover and dependent workflow conditions.

- ✓ Postive Conditions
- ✓ Negative Conditions
- ✓ Boundary Conditions
- ✓ workflow Conditions
- ✓ Security Conditions
- ✓ Performance Conditions
- ✓ Failover Conditions

As team, we need to understand our NFRs. In today environment, the list of NFRs are heavy and team needs to ensure these NFRs are addressed as part of framework and product intrinsic requirements.

Testing team needs to ensure different types of testing are considered as part of test strategy and approach. It is expected in agile team the testing may not happen just once rather more in iterative and incremental manner based on products increments over sprints.

This situation causes to investigate strategy of mixing functional and regression at each incremental and requesting for automations and manual for better agility in teams based on requirements volatility.

> Functional Testing
> Regression Testing
> Performance Testing
> Security Testing
> Readiness Testing
> Failover Testing

As for Testing team in agile projects, the testers should be equipped with skills and tools to be more agile and increase agility to meet timeline and product quality. It is imperative we follow some standard recommendation as listed below:

1. Please make sure test case are written and completed for end-2-end flow from user point or interaction, following BDD practices helps in filling gaps.
2. Please ensure user stories are grouped as per end-2-end flow and are executed in set rather in isolation. Here, we need to ensure all end-2-end flow or BDD conditions are executed in set to cover all condition in defined or planned priority.
3. While executing
   a. Please ensure first positive end-2-end flow are verified and validated– any blockers to be considering to be highest priority - High
   b. If positive flow is passed – Please execute end-2end flow for Negative & Security conditions as Medium priority

   Once flow is passed, it's time to focus on page level validation.
   1. Error validation
   2. Data validation
   3. Boundary conditions
   4. Responsive
   5. Accessibility

It is always good to give more importance to user interaction flow as top priority, since they are user behaviors. If team can complete flow, it means customer can perform actions without impacting.

However, it is also equally necessary to ensure our page field, error and boundary and other conditions are validated for better customer experience and overall quality.

Agility in Support and Deployment

Development, Release, and Deployment Concepts

There are several terms related to the development, release, and deployment of software that have not previously been covered in the definitions of the methodologies discussed so far in this chapter. These are concepts that describe the how's of developing and deploying software and understanding what they are and how they relate will give readers a more mature understanding of how tools can be used to facilitate these practices down the line.

Version Control

A version control system records changes to files or sets of files stored within the system. This can be source code, assets, and other documents that may be part of a software development project. Developers make changes in groups called commits or revisions. Each revision, along with metadata such as who made the change and when, is stored within the system in one way or another. Having the ability to commit, compare, merge, and restore past revisions to objects to the repository allows for richer cooperation and collaboration within and between teams. It minimizes risks by establishing a way to revert objects in production to previous versions.

Application Deployment

Application deployment is the process of planning, maintaining, and executing on the delivery of a software release. In the general sense, the craft of application deployment needs to consider the changes that are taking place underneath the system. Having infrastructure automation build the dependencies required to run a specific application—whether they be computing, operating system, or other dependencies— minimizes the impact of inconsistencies on the released software. Depending on the application type, different engineering concerns may be important. For example, databases may have strict guarantees in terms of consistency. If a transaction occurs, it must be reflected in the data. Application deployment is a critical aspect to engineering quality software.

Continuous Integration

Continuous integration (CI) is the process of integrating new code written by developers with a mainline or "master" branch frequently throughout the day. This contrasts with having developers working on independent feature branches for weeks or months at a time, merging their code back to the master branch only when it is finished. Long periods of time in between merges means that much more has been changed, increasing the likelihood of some of those changes being breaking ones. With bigger changesets, it is much more difficult to isolate and identify what caused something to break. With small, frequently merged changesets, finding the specific change that caused a regression is much easier. The goal is to avoid the kinds of integration problems that come from large, infrequent merges. To make sure that the integrations were successful, CI systems will usually run a series of tests automatically upon merging in new changes. When these changes are committed and merged, the tests automatically start running to avoid the overhead of people having to remember to run them—the more overhead an activity requires, the less likely it is that it will get done, especially when people are in a hurry. The outcome of these tests is often visualized, where "green" means the tests passed and the newly integrated build is considered clean and failing or "red" tests means the build is broken and needs to be fixed. With this kind of workflow, problems can be identified and fixed much more quickly.

This process followed in development team ensure all team to know on how each team member is contributing towards overall product development on daily basis and challenges being faced. It helps team to know disconnected flow in products despite build being successful.

This process allows team to be in sync with team's contribution on daily basis and forces to some of best practices and provides agility in resolving integration and quality issues of product or product components.

It helps team codes to be up-to-date and streamlines build and release to various servers increasing team productivity.

Not always every team gets full server stack for its development, there are challenges in getting multiple servers for each stages of development life cycle.

In such cases, it is recommended, that one of development server of team members is converted to consists of integrated codes before other releasing to other environments.

It also helps central governance and validating requirements and running test scripts against integrated servers usually called as System Integration environment towards quality delivery from development team to QA team.

Continuous Delivery

Continuous delivery (CD) is a set of general software engineering principles that allow for frequent releases of new software using automated testing and continuous integration. It is closely related to CI and is often thought of as taking CI one step further, that beyond simply making sure that new changes can be integrated without causing regressions to automated tests, continuous delivery means that these changes can be deployed.

Today, we have automation products or tools helping in achieving maximum agility for agile team. Some of well-known tools are VSTS DevOps and Octopus used in CI/CD process.

The Dev-Ops framework focus primarily on these practices to ensure quality deliverables reach out to customers on quick interval and ae used by many organizations in product support (Level-2)

We might at time take it easy or get into assumption all is good as we are following best practices in build and release, however it is proved time and again that if we do not perform adequate sanity check it results in quality issues. It is always better for dev team to perform sanity or smoke check on dev and QA environment once code has been released or patched to ensure all is working as expected.

It is also important for team supporting in production application to follow strategy for BLUE-GREEN approach to ensure new release does not impact customer due to upgrade.

Continuous Deployment

Continuous deployment (also referred to as CD) is the process of deploying changes to production by defining tests and validations to minimize risk. While continuous delivery makes sure that new changes can be deployed, continuous deployment means that they get deployed into production. The more quickly software changes make it into production, the sooner individuals see their work in effect. Visibility of work impact increases job satisfaction, and overall happiness with work, leading to higher performance. It also provides opportunities to learn more quickly. If something is fundamentally wrong with a design or feature, the context of work is more recent and easier to reason about and change. Continuous deployment also gets the product out to the customer faster, which can mean increased customer satisfaction (though it should be noted that this is not a panacea—customers won't appreciate getting an updated product if that update doesn't solve any of their problems, so you must make sure through other methods that you are building the right thing). This can mean validating its success or failure faster as well, allowing teams and organizations to iterate and change more rapidly as needed.

PART C

Rise of Frameworks

During the early stage of software development, the team focused on business automation. They helped users to provide services much quicker and cut operating expenses.

First, the development team came up with a sequential process representing development phases. This model was a waterfall.

The sequential process enabled the team to build and deliver better software. Only a few players in markets developed and released products for customers.

Years later, many players entered the development market resulting in more competition. At the same time, industries were struggling to manage finances and to cut expenses. The demand for software products to deliver at less cost and quicker were in great demand.

A new process was soon identified to build software products in incremental. This process was IID - Iterative and incremental development process. The IID helped the development team to understand customer priorities in product construction. It prevented customer rejections and increased adoptions.

As market dynamics became more competitive, companies required better and improved methods. They had to improve performance and reduce wastages to run at profits. Products required quicker development and changes to fight competition and grab market shares.

Throughput process and methods helped to meet these demands. These new process and methods called a lean process. It became popular and its adoption increased in the corporates.

The lean influenced all professionals across industries and gave rise to new frameworks. Each framework brought in agility to respective practices in industries. Product development became much easier and quicker. They also avoided common conflicts and confusion within teams.

After improving functional agility, the team agility gave birth to agile team processes. The new agile team process resulted in the rise of life cycle frameworks to improve team agility. These frameworks extended domain or functional frameworks for better team results.

Soon, timeboxing of development resulted in the scrum. Timeboxing (iteration with fixed length) reduced lead and cycle time. It insisted the team to focus on customer interactions and business values. More regular reviews and retrospective promoted in quality delivery with satisfied customers.

Domain Frameworks

During early days of process evolution in software development to meet customer demands. The software team required better ways to avoid ambiguity in information communicated. They need to control and avoid reworks that caused delays.

No longer Sequential or Iterative and Incremental model was enough for development teams. These models did not solve the gaps in customer priorities shared with the sales team. The development team hardly interacted with customers. The final product took longer time than expected due to rework and customer mismatch.

The specification required more frequent updates to agreed incremental sets. Information loss during handover transition caused a lot of confusions within the team. It resulted in missing deadlines and incorrect product delivery.

The product manager struggled to maintain plans due to constant changes and gaps. The plan approvals were taking much longer and delayed deadlines and milestones.

They required a method to handle constant changes in schedule and allocation. The PDCA process and methods gave required relief to handle changes in plans. The new planning process focused on continuous improvements by following plan-do-check-act activities.

The wave plan practices became much common as it aligned to Incremental developments. It helped project managers to identify risks and issues for ongoing commitments. it enables to be more adaptive to ongoing changes.

The development team came with new team communication and development practices with models. The model engineering saved long interaction times and reduced textual content in specifications. This gave birth to MDE methods and practices for developers in the software industry. The UML further standardize robust design communication with many teams. They reduce conflicts and understanding of what and how to build the right products. The MDE improved the agility of TA and Analyst to accommodate change requests.

The JAD session became more common with development testing with customers.

The visual over textual content took preference. It aligned team members and minimized ambiguity. The design model enabled the development team to deliver without any major issues.

The improved innovation in the development and planning process influenced other team members. The practices and skills enabled technical team to interact with customer teams. The change resulted in new business analyst roles to evolve and focusing requirements. They bridged gaps between customers and technical teams.

The next major challenges faced by the technical team was customer requirements. Many customers were not sure what they wanted, this resulted in prototype methods. Soon, it evolved to RAD framework boosting development team productivity.

RAD helped in developing product much faster meeting customer expectation. At times, it resulted in more design and code rework. A new pairing process helped in reducing some of the rework as changes demanded in products.

As the need for adapting to changes were inevitable, design and code changes became a must. As prototypes focused to understand customer needs and not functional product, refactoring evolved.

This new process and methods gave rise to Extreme programming (XP) frameworks. Many more technical frameworks and methods evolved for developers to construct code faster.

The requirements professionals did face a lot of challenges in getting customer needs. They were more conflicts seen between the technical team and functional team. The improved gathering and elicitation process did not add value to the technical team. This resulted in applying some standard techniques technical team applied to design modelling. The grouping of requirements focused on domain or service resulted in better alignment. This new benefit moved towards the formation of FDD framework. Feature Driven Development (FDD) embraced earlier agile methods. It evolved to life cycle frameworks, but unsuccessful due to acceptance.

As importance increased towards responsive, scalability, performance and security, Quality became more important.

The agile methods were complementing requirements team and development team. The testing team need an improved process to get aligned with the rest. Traceability to requirements was missing and better practices required to increase speed. The FDD influenced testing experts and soon BDD got rolled out.

BDD framework improved traceability and complemented user stories focused on features and epics. It enabled the development team, aligned design and test team with common principles.

As time evolved, challenges increased, and innovation came around. The support professional challenges in getting hotfixes to customers resulted in DevOps.

The DevOps forced to support and development team to work together as one team. instead of working in silos. It allowed technical and business team to work towards common goals. It embraced the CI/CD process to improve the agility of the support team.

Many times, the operational challenges in team resulted in incorrect product delivery. At times due to challenges in rework and quality issues, deadlines got missed. It resulted in customer dissatisfaction.

The customer was insisting to become more open and involve earlier to get the right product on time. The focus shifted towards existing Lifecycle models or team process like a waterfall, IID, Spiral, V-Model, etc...

The team process acted as a bottleneck for team speed in reaching to customers. It was acting as a weak link of team and breaking team agility. The experts soon decided to strengthen the team process to improve the agility of the team.

This focus on team process resulted in agile life-cycle frameworks. Many frameworks were an extension of domain framework and methods. They failed due to disagreements between cross-functional teams based on specialization and adoptions.

The outcome forced experts to come with better team models and frameworks. Adding time limits to traditional models, agility got increased. This resulted in a new agile team process and frameworks.

As expected, first to bang and erupt was Scrum. Soon followed by SOS, LeSS, SAFe, Nexus and DAD.

Agile Plan Framework

Plan-Do-Check-Act cycle is a model for carrying out change. It is an essential part of the lean manufacturing philosophy and a key prerequisite for continuous improvement of people and processes.

It is used for a new product or concept development, problem solving, project implementation and many other fields.

DMAIC refers to a data-driven quality strategy for improving processes and is an integral part of the company's Six Sigma Quality Initiative. DMAIC is an acronym for five interconnected phases: Define, Measure, Analyze, Improve, and Control.

The goal of A3 Planning is to put all relevant facts regarding a plan on one piece of paper and be able to tell the story about the plan as quickly and succinctly as possible.

The Eight Disciplines of Problem Solving (8D) is a problem-solving methodology designed to find the root cause of a problem, devise a short-term fix and implement a long-term solution to prevent recurring problems.

1D	• Team formation
2D	• Problem Description
3D	• Interim containment Actions
4D	• Root Cause Analysis
5D	• Corrective Actions
6D	• Validate Corrective Actions
7D	• Identify & Implement Preventive Actions
8D	• Team & Individual Recognition

Agile Requirements Framework

FDD was designed to follow a five-step development process, built largely around discrete "feature" projects based on user interactions.

1. Develop an overall model
2. Build a features list
3. Plan by feature
4. Design by feature
5. Build by feature

- Process one – develop an overall model: The FDD model insists that teams exert the adequate amount of effort at the start of the project to build an object model highlighting the domain problem.
  Modelling with feature driven development is time-boxed and collaborative. Domain models should be created in detail by small groups and then presented for peers to review. It is hoped that a proposed model – or potentially a combination of them – will then be used for each area of the domain. They will then be merged over time to produce an overall model.
- Process two – build a feature list: From the knowledge that is obtained during the modelling process, a list of features is established by dividing domains into subject areas that contain information on business activities. The steps that are used for each business activity represent a categorized list of features. Features are

RAD model is Rapid Application Development model. It is a type of incremental model. In RAD model the components or functions are developed in parallel as if they were mini projects. The developments are time boxed, delivered and then assembled into a working prototype.

The Prototyping Model is a systems development method (SDM) in which a prototype (an early approximation of a final system or product) is built, tested, and then reworked as necessary until an acceptable prototype is finally achieved from which the complete system or product can now be developed.

Agile Design Framework

MDF – Model Driven Engineering Framework

As the strategic value of software increases for many companies, the industry looks for techniques to automate the production of software and to improve quality and reduce cost and time-to-market. These techniques include component technology, visual programming, patterns and frameworks. Businesses also seek techniques to manage the complexity of systems as they increase in scope and scale. They recognize the need to solve recurring architectural problems, such as physical distribution, concurrency, replication, security, load balancing and fault tolerance

UML, short for Unified Modeling Language, is a standardized modeling language consisting of an integrated set of diagrams, developed to help system and software developers for specifying, visualizing, constructing, and documenting the artifacts of software systems, as well as for business modeling and other non-software systems. The UML represents a collection of best engineering practices that have proven successful in the modeling of large and complex systems. The UML is a very important part of developing object-oriented software and the software development process. The UML uses mostly graphical notations to express the design of software projects. Using the UML helps project teams communicate, explore potential designs, and validate the architectural design of the software. In this article we will give you detailed ideas about what is UML, the history of UML and a description of each UML diagram type, along with UML examples.

The first thing to notice about the UML is that there are a lot of different diagrams (models) to get used to. The reason for this n for this is that it is possible to look at a system from many different viewpoints. A software development will have many stakeholders playing a part.

For Example:

- Analysts
- Designers
- Coders
- Testers
- QA
- The Customer
- Technical Authors

1. Provide users with a ready-to-use, expressive visual modeling language so they can develop and exchange meaningful models.
2. Provide extensibility and specialization mechanisms to extend the core concepts.
3. Be independent of programming languages and development processes.
4. Provide a formal basis for understanding the modeling language.
5. Encourage the growth of the OO tools market.
6. Support higher-level development concepts such as collaborations, frameworks, patterns and components.

7. Integrate best practices.

Structure diagrams show the static structure of the system and its parts on different abstraction and implementation levels and how they are related to each other. The elements in a structure diagram represent the meaningful concepts of a system, and may include abstract, real world and implementation concepts, there are seven types of structure diagram as follows:

- Class Diagram
- Component Diagram
- Deployment Diagram
- Object Diagram
- Package Diagram
- Composite Structure Diagram
- Profile Diagram

Behavior diagrams show the dynamic behavior of the objects in a system, which can be described as a series of changes to the system over time, there are seven types of behavior diagrams as follows:

- Use Case Diagram
- Activity Diagram
- State Machine Diagram
- Sequence Diagram
- Communication Diagram
- Interaction Overview Diagram
- Timing Diagram

Agile Code frameworks

CC – Clean Code Framework Method.

Clean code:

Clean code is focused on best practices in industry to provide maximum benefits towards readability, reusability, extendibility and maintainability.

1. It should be elegant — Clean code should be *pleasing* to read. Reading it should make you smile the way a well-crafted music box or well-designed car would.
2. Clean code is focused —Each function, each class, each module exposes a single-minded attitude that remains entirely undistracted, and unpolluted, by the surrounding details.
3. Clean code is taken care of. Someone has taken the time to keep it simple and orderly. They have paid appropriate attention to details. They have cared.
4. Runs all the tests
5. Contains no duplication
6. Minimize the number of entities such as classes, methods, functions, and the like.

Some practices followed in clean codes are mentioned below:

KISS: Keep It Simple Stupid. A design principle originating from the U.S. Navy that goes back to 1960 already. It states that most systems should be kept as simple as possible, Unnecessary complexity should be avoided.

DRY: Don't Repeat Yourself. Closely related to KISS and the minimalist design philosophy. It states that every piece of knowledge (code, in this case) must have a single, unambiguous, authoritative representation within a system (codebase). Violations of DRY are referred to as WET: We Enjoy Typing, Write Everything Twice, Waste Everyone's Time.

YAGNI: You Aren't Going to Need It. A developer should not add functionality unless deemed necessary. YAGNI is part of the Extreme Programming (XP) methodology, which wants to improve software quality and increase responsiveness to customer requirements. YAGNI should be used in conjunction with continuous refactoring, unit testing, and integration.

Composition over inheritance: Not an acronym, sadly. It's a principle where you design your types over what they do instead of over what they are. Composition is favored over inheritance by many developers, because inheritance forces you to build a taxonomy of objects early on in a project, making your code inflexible for changes later.

Favor readability: It's not because a machine can read your code that another human can. Particularly when working with multiple people on a project, always favor readability over conciseness. There's no point in having concise code if people don't understand it.

Practice consistency: This is arguably the overarching principle of all clean code principles. If you decide to do something a certain way, stick to it throughout the entire project. If you have no choice but to move away from your original choice, explain why in the comments.

XP – Extreme Programming Framework Method.

Extreme Programming (XP) is an agile software development framework that aims to produce higher quality software, and higher quality of life for the development team. XP is the most specific of the agile frameworks regarding appropriate engineering practices for software development.

The five values of XP are communication, simplicity, feedback, courage, and respect and are described in more detail below.

Communication

Software development is inherently a team sport that relies on communication to transfer knowledge from one team member to everyone else on the team. XP stresses the importance of the appropriate kind of communication - face to face discussion with the aid of a white board or other drawing mechanism.

Simplicity

Simplicity means "what is the simplest thing that will work?" The purpose of this is to avoid waste and do only necessary things such as keep the design of the system as simple as possible so that it is easier to maintain, support, and revise. Simplicity also means address only the requirements that you know about; don't try to predict the future.

Feedback

Through constant feedback about their previous efforts, teams can identify areas for improvement and revise their practices. Feedback also supports simple design. Your team builds something, gathers feedback on your design and implementation, and then adjust your product going forward.

Courage

Preference for action based on other principles so that the results aren't harmful to the team. You need courage to raise organizational issues that reduce your team's effectiveness. You need courage to stop doing something that doesn't work and try something else. You need courage to accept and act on feedback, even when it's difficult to accept.

Respect

The members of your team need to respect each other to communicate with each other, provide and accept feedback that honors your relationship, and to work together to identify simple designs and solutions.

CI – Continuous Integration Framework Method.

Continuous Integration (CI) is a development practice that requires developers to integrate code into a shared repository several times a day. Each check-in is then verified by an automated build, allowing teams to detect problems early.

To achieve these objectives, continuous integration relies on the following principles.

Maintain a code repository

This practice advocates the use of a revision control system for the project's source code. All artifacts required to build the project should be placed in the repository. In this practice and in the revision control community, the convention is that the system should be buildable from a fresh checkout and not require additional dependencies.

Build automation

A single command should have the capability of building the system and Make the build self-testing. Once the code is built, all tests should run to confirm that it behaves as the developers expect it to behave

Everyone commits to the baseline every day

By committing regularly, every committer can reduce the number of conflicting changes. Checking in a week's worth of work runs the risk of conflicting with other features and can be very difficult to resolve. Early, small conflicts in an area of the system cause team members to communicate about the change they are making.

Every commit (to baseline) should be built

The system should build commits to the current working version to verify that they integrate correctly. A common practice is to use Automated Continuous Integration, although this may be done manually. Automated Continuous Integration employs a continuous integration server to monitor the revision control system for changes, then automatically run the build process.

Keep the build fast

The build needs to complete rapidly, so that if there is a problem with integration, it is quickly identified.

Test in a clone of the production environment

Having a test environment can lead to failures in tested systems when they deploy in the production environment because the production environment may differ from the test environment in a significant way.

A separate pre-production environment ("staging") should be built to be a scalable version of the production environment and obtain on-demand access to dependencies (e.g., APIs, third-party applications, services, etc.) that are beyond the team's control, still evolving, and is likely to part of production system.

Make it easy to get the latest deliverables

Making builds readily available to stakeholders and testers can reduce the amount of rework necessary when rebuilding a feature that doesn't meet requirements. Additionally, early testing reduces the chances that defects survive until deployment. Finding errors earlier can reduce the amount of work necessary to resolve them.

All programmers should start the day by updating the project from the repository. That way, they will all stay up to date.

Everyone can see the results of the latest build

It should be easy to find out whether the build breaks and, if so, who made the relevant change and what that change was.

Automate deployment

Most CI systems allow the running of scripts after a build finish. In most situations, it is possible to write a script to deploy the application to a live test server that everyone can look at. A further advance in this way of thinking is continuous deployment, which calls for the software to be deployed directly into production, often with additional automation to prevent defects or regressions.

Agile Test Frameworks

Test Driven Development

TDD can be defined as a programming practice that instructs developers to write new code only if an automated test has failed. This avoids duplication of code. TDD means "Test Driven Development". The primary goal of TDD is to make the code clearer, simple and bug-free.

Test-Driven Development starts with designing and developing tests for every small functionality of an application. In TDD approach, first, the test is developed which specifies and validates what the code will do. The process is more common with developers and is adopted as part of coding phase rather in testing phase.

In the normal Software Testing process, we first generate the code and then test. Tests might fail since tests are developed even before the development. To pass the test, the development team must develop and refactors the code. Refactoring a code means changing some code without affecting its behavior.

The simple concept of TDD is to write and correct the failed tests before writing new code (before development). This helps to avoid duplication of code as we write a small amount of code at a time to pass tests. (Tests are nothing but requirement conditions that we need to test to fulfill them).

Test-Driven development is a process of developing and running automated test before actual development of the application. Hence, TDD sometimes also called as Test First Development.

Two levels of TDD

1. Acceptance TDD (ATDD): With ATDD you write a single acceptance test. This test fulfills the requirement of the specification or satisfies the behavior of the system. After that write just enough, production/functionality code to fulfill that acceptance test. Acceptance test focuses on the overall behavior of the system. ATDD also was known as Behavioral Driven Development (BDD).
2. Developer TDD: With Developer TDD you write single developer test i.e. unit test and then just enough production code to fulfill that test. The unit test focuses on every small functionality of the system. Developer TDD is simply called as TDD.
   The main goal of ATDD and TDD is to specify detailed, executable requirements for your solution on a just in time (JIT) basis. JIT means taking only those requirements in consideration that are needed in the system.

Behavior Driven Development

Behavior Driven testing is an extension of TDD. Like in TDD in BDD also we write tests first and the add application code. The major difference that we get to see here are

- *Tests are written in plain descriptive English type grammar*
- *Tests are explained as behavior of application and are more user focused*
- *Using examples to clarify requirements*

This difference brings in the need to have a language which can define, in an understandable format.

Features of BDD
1. *Shifting from thinking in "tests" to thinking in "behavior"*
2. *Collaboration between Business stakeholders, Business Analysts, QA Team and developers*
3. *Ubiquitous language, it is easy to describe*
4. *Driven by Business Value*
5. *Extends Test Driven Development (TDD) by utilizing natural language that non-technical stakeholders can understand*

An Example of BDD

Feature: Sign up

Scenario: As user, I should be able to Sign up, so that I can access product functionalities or features.

Condition: Successful sign up

> *Given I have chosen to sign up*
> *When I sign up with valid details*
> *Then I should receive a confirmation email*
> *And I should see a personalized greeting message*

Condition: Duplicate email

> *Given I have chosen to sign up*
> *But I enter an email address that has already registered*
> *Then I should be told that the email is already registered*
> *And I should be offered the option to recover my password*

Agile Support & Deployment Frameworks

DevOps is the blending of the team development and operations, meant to represent a collaborative or shared approach to the tasks performed by a company's application development and IT operations teams.

The term DevOps is used in several ways. In its most broad meaning, DevOps is an operational philosophy that promotes better communication between these teams -- and others. In its most narrow interpretation, DevOps describes the adoption of automation and programmable software development and infrastructure deployment and maintenance.

DevOps is not a technology, there include continuous integration and continuous delivery or continuous deployment tools, with an emphasis on task automation. Other products to support DevOps include real-time monitoring and incident response systems as well as collaboration platforms.

It arose from the success in the speed of development in Agile, when it became clear that there is a lack of communication between development and operations teams that put a significant hindrance on speed and flexibility of code delivery to users.

Lifecycle Frameworks

As the focus to find better frameworks to manage software development end to end. The first to roll-out based on new lean process and practices were DSDM, MSF and UP.

The DSDM focused prototyping and best practices of RAD process and methods. It promoted flexibility and clarity in software construction methods. It also embraced lean practices for cost-effective development.

But, they were challenges to prototype, since prototyping did not help in all contexts. It turned out to be more of a burden to a few teams and non-acceptance were getting increased. They prefer to adopt traditional models like a waterfall for less complex scenarios.

Yet, since it did not improve the team agility, the experts looked out for better frameworks. They required speed and quality without compromising on scope, time and cost. The Kanban board were becoming very popular. TQM (Total Quality Management) and TPM (Total Productivity Management) adoptions challenged experts.

It took time to rollout team process complementing the lean process. A new team process with time limit for life cycle phases got proposed. This new process soon became popular as Scrum. It enabled more frequent interaction, retrospective and reviews with customer and stakeholders.

The above process became popular and got adopted by the technical team. The scrum framework focused on the team and became a better life cycle model. Timeboxing, retrospective and short standups complemented in better team interaction and bonding. Promoting ownership, self-organizing and collaboration resulted in quicker and boost innovation.

The scrum became default agile life cycle frameworks for the team. It further evolved to support large teams. Frameworks like LeSS, Scrum of Scrum, SAFe and DAD rolled out supporting large team size.

Lack of agile organizational team process resulted in frameworks like SAFe and DAD. The new frameworks enabled external teams like pre-sales, sales, support and operations. They even embraced other agile frameworks to benefit the organization and corporate teams.

DAD team embraced more on IID, Unified Process, RAD, scrum and other lean processes. DAD accommodated matrix roles against agile artefacts. Here, the team owns artefacts like backlogs made up of Epic, features and stories.

SAFe embraced value-chains, XP, dev-ops and Kanban. The artefacts got mapped against portfolios (Epics), programs (features) and projects (user stories). It mandates at artefacts level and enforces agile practices at the organization level.

Dynamic System Development Methods

DSDM is an Agile method that focuses on the full project lifecycle. Project managers using Rapid Application Development sought more governance and discipline. Because of this need, this new iterative way of working DSDM came into existence. DSDM (known as Dynamic System Development Method) was created in 1994.

The method provides a four-phase framework consisting of:

- Feasibility and business study
- Functional model / prototype iteration
- Design and build iteration
- Implementation

The eight Principles of DSDM:

- Focus on the business need
- Deliver on time
- Collaborate
- Never compromise quality
- Build incrementally from firm foundations
- Develop iteratively
- Communicate continuously and clearly
- Demonstrate control

DSDM is vendor-independent, covers the entire life-cycle of a project. DSDM provides best practice guidance for on-time, on-budget delivery of projects. It has the proven scalability to address projects of all sizes and for any business sector.

DSDM advocates the use of several proven practices, including:

- Facilitated Workshops
- Modelling and Iterative Development

- MoSCoW Prioritization
- Time boxing

The term MoSCoW itself is an acronym of four prioritization categories- Must have, should have, could have, and Won't have. While the Os are usually in lower-case to or show that they do not stand for anything, the all-capitals MOSCOW is also used. DSDM is designed to be easily tailored and used in conjunction with traditional methods such as PRINCE2® or to complement other Agile approaches such as Scrum.

DSDM is designed to be easily tailored and used in conjunction with traditional methods. DSDM complements methods such as PRINCE2® or to complement other Agile approaches such as Scrum.

Each phase of DSDM relies on several different activities and techniques based on the below principles:

Projects evolve best through direct and co-located collaboration between the developers and the users.

Self-managed and empowered teams must have the authority to make time sensitive and critical project-level decisions.

Design and development are incremental and evolutionary in nature and is largely driven by regular, iterative user feedback.

Working software deliverables are defined as systems that address the critical, current business needs versus systems that address less critical future needs.

Frequent and incremental delivery of working software is valued over infrequent delivery of perfectly working software.

All changes introduced during development must be reversible.

Continuous integration and quality assurance testing are conducted in-line, throughout the project lifecycle.

Visibility and transparency are encouraged through regular communication and collaboration amongst all project stakeholders.

Scrum

Scrum is a framework that helps teams work together. Scrum encourages teams to learn through experiences, self-organize while working on a problem, and continuously improve.

Its principles can be applied to all kinds of teamwork. This is one of the reasons Scrum is so popular.

SCRUM is not an acronym. It was named after rugby's scrum. Scrum is a light framework with only a few key rules and a limited set of practices.

Benefits of Scrum:

- Risk Mitigation due to faster feedback cycles.
- Reduced time-to-market hence improved ROI (return on investment)
- Improved Stakeholders satisfaction
- Confidence to succeed in a complex product development.

Scrum team consists of three roles:

- Product owner: The most empowered central point of product leadership.
- Scrum Master: Acts as a coach, providing process leadership, helping the Scrum team. Scrum Master also helps the organization develop its organization-specific Scrum approach.
- Development team: A cross-function team which handles designing, building, and testing the desired product.

Scrum has three Artefacts:

- Product backlog
- Sprint backlog
- Potentially shippable product

Activities:

- Sprint planning
- Daily scrum
- Sprint review
- Sprint retrospective

One of the important activities which is commonly practiced in Scrum is Product backlog grooming

Kanban

Kanban is a visual system for managing work as it moves through a process. Kanban visualizes both the process (the workflow) and the actual work passing through that process. The goal of Kanban is to identify potential bottlenecks in your process and fix them. This enables the workflow through it cost-effectively at optimal speed or throughput.

A Kanban system ideally controls the entire value chain from the supplier to the end consumer. In this way, it helps avoid supply disruption and overstocking of goods at various stages of the manufacturing process. Kanban requires continuous monitoring of the process. Attention needs to be given to avoid bottlenecks that could slow down the production process. The aim is to achieve higher throughput with lower delivery lead times. Over time, Kanban has become an efficient way in a variety of production systems.

The Kanban Method follows a set of principles and practices for managing and improving the flow of work. It is an evolutionary, non-disruptive method. Kanban promotes gradual improvements to an organization's processes. If you follow these principles and practices, you will be able to use Kanban for maximizing the benefits to your business process. This will help improve flow, reduce cycle time, increase value to the customer. These all are crucial to any business today.

The four foundational principles and six Core Practices of the Kanban Methodology are provided below:

Foundational Principles

- <u>Start with what you are doing now</u>: The Kanban Method emphasizes not making any change to your existing setup/ process right away. Kanban must be applied directly to the current workflow. Any changes needed can occur gradually over a period at a pace the team is comfortable with.
- <u>Agree to pursue incremental, evolutionary change:</u> Kanban encourages you to make small incremental changes. Making radical changes that might lead to resistance within the team and organization.
- <u>Respect current roles, responsibilities and job-titles:</u> Unlike other methods, Kanban does not impose any organizational changes by itself. So, it is not necessary to make changes to your existing roles and functions which may be performing well. The team will collaboratively identify and implement any changes needed. These principles help the organizations overcome the emotional resistance and the fear of change.
- <u>Encourage acts of leadership at all levels:</u> Kanban encourages continuous improvement at all the levels of the organization. and it says that leadership acts don't have to originate from senior managers only. People at all levels can provide ideas and show leadership to implement changes. This will continually improve the way they deliver their products and services.

Core Practices of the Kanban Method

Visualize the flow of work: This is the fundamental first step to adopting and implementing the Kanban Method. You need to visualize the process steps that you currently use to deliver your work or your services. Depending on the complexity of your process and your work-mix, your Kanban board can be very simple to very elaborate. Once you visualize your process, then you can visualize the current work that you and your team are doing.

Limit WIP (Work in Progress): Limiting work-in-progress is fundamental to implementing Kanban – a 'Pull-system'. By limiting WIP, you encourage your team to complete work at hand first before taking up new work. Thus, work currently in progress must be completed and marked done. This creates capacity in the system, so new work can be pulled in by the team.

Manage Flow: Managing and improving flow is the crux of your Kanban system after you have implemented the first 2 practices. A Kanban system helps you manage flow by highlighting the various stages of the workflow and the status of work in each stage. Depending on how well the workflow is defined and WIP Limits are set, you will observe either a smooth flow of work piling up as something gets held up. All this affects how quickly work traverses from start to the end of the workflow (some people call it value stream). Kanban helps your team analyze the system and adjust improve flow to reduce the time it takes to complete each piece of work.

Make Process Policies Explicit: As part of visualizing the process, it makes sense to also define and visualize policies. Create a common basis for all participants to understand how to do any type of work in the system. The policies can be at the board level, at a swim lane level and for each column. They can be a checklist of steps to be done for each work item type. Entry-exit criteria for each column, or anything at all that helps team members manage the flow of work on the board well.

Implement Feedback Loops: Feedback loops are an integral part of any good system. The Kanban Method encourages and helps implement feedback loops. Review stages in Kanban board workflow, metrics and reports provide continuous feedback on work progress – or the lack of it – in the system.

Improve Collaboratively, Evolve Experimentally: The Kanban Method is an evolutionary improvement process. It helps you adopt small changes and improve gradually at a pace and size that your team can handle easily. It encourages the use of the scientific method – forms a hypothesis, tests it and makes changes depending on the outcome of the test. The key task of a team implementing Lean/ Agile principles is to evaluate process constantly and improve continuously.

The concept of FLOW

At the core of Kanban is the concept of "Flow". This means that the cards should flow through the system as evenly as possible, without long waiting times or blockages. Everything that hinders the flow should be critically examined. Kanban has different techniques, metrics and models. If these are consistently applied, can lead to a culture of continuous improvement (kaizen).

The concept of Flow is critical. Measuring and improving flow metrics can dramatically improve the speed of delivery processes. This also improves the quality of products or services by getting faster feedback from customers.

Disciplined Agile Delivery

Disciplined Agile Delivery (DAD) is a people-first, hybrid agile approach to IT solution delivery. It has a risk-value delivery lifecycle, is goal-driven, is enterprise aware, and is scalable.

DAD promotes a full delivery lifecycle and defines three explicit phases. These phases are Inception, Construction, Transition.

- Inception: Where you initiate the project.
- Construction: Where you build/configure the solution.
- Transition: Where you deploy the solution into production or the marketplace.

DAD picks up where Scrum leaves off. DAD describes how all agile techniques fit together, going far beyond Scrum, to define a full agile solution delivery lifecycle. Like Scrum the DAD addresses leadership, roles & responsibilities, and requirements change management. Unlike Scrum DAD doesn't stop there, it also addresses other important aspects of software development such as architecture, design, testing, programming, documentation, deployment and many more. In short, DAD provides a much broader understanding of how agile development works in practice, doing a lot of the "heavy process lifting" that Scrum leaves up to you.

DAD is pragmatic. The DA toolkit provides choices, not prescriptions, enabling you to easily tailor a strategy that reflects the situation that your team finds itself in. To do this effectively you need to understand the process-oriented choices you have and what the trade-offs are. DAD makes these choices explicit through its process-goal driven approach.

DAD supports both lean and agile ways of working (WoW). DAD supports several delivery lifecycles, including a Scrum-based agile lifecycle, a Kanban-based lean lifecycle, two continuous delivery lifecycles, a Lean Startup-based exploratory lifecycle, and a Program "team of teams" lifecycle. Teams find themselves in unique situations, and as a result one process size does not fit all. Even in small companies we've seen situations where some teams are taking an agile approach, some a lean approach, and some combinations thereof.

DAD is based on empiricism. For several years Scott Ambler, Mark Lines, and many other contributors to DAD worked in or visited hundreds of enterprises around the world in a wide range of industries and environments. DAD, and the DA toolkit in general, captures the proven strategies adopted by these organizations, describing the strengths and weaknesses of each strategy and providing guidance for when and when not to apply them.

DAD provides a solid foundation from which to scale agile. DAD supports successful scaling of agile and lean techniques in several ways. First, its full delivery lifecycles and breadth of software development advice answers how to successfully apply agile in practice. Second, its goal driven approach provides the required flexibility for tailoring your agile process to meet the challenges faced by agile teams working at scale. Third, DAD builds in many foundational concepts required at scale, including DevOps, explicit agile governance, and enterprise awareness.

DAD enables and goes beyond SAFe. SAFe leaves the details of construction to you and as a result can prove to be fragile in many organizations. DAD provides the solid process foundation missing from SAFe and is in fact complementary to SAFe. DAD describes several strategies for organizing large or geographically distributed teams. It describes a range of options for scaling your approach to agile and lean software development, giving you context-sensitive options that SAFe doesn't.

DAD teams deliver solutions, not just software. DAD recognizes that the software we develop runs on hardware, which may need upgrades, and it is supported by documentation. Our stakeholders may also need to evolve their business processes, and sometimes even their organization structures, to address the new needs of the situation that they face. In short, DAD teams deliver solutions that comprise software, hardware changes, supporting documentation, improved business processes, and even organizational changes.

DAD is evolving. We're constantly learning as practitioners, learning about and experimenting with new agile and lean strategies all the time. These learnings are constantly being applied to evolve DAD.

There are several ways that DAD differs from Scrum:
1. Greater lifecycle breadth. DAD supports a full delivery lifecycle, going beyond Scrum's construction lifecycle to also provide advice for how to effectively initiate an agile project (or product) and how to transition/release into production. In other words, it helps take some of the mystery out of how all this agile stuff works in practice.
2. Focus on enterprise awareness. A strength of Scrum is its inward focus within a project team to minimize distractions and thus enabling the team to focus on delivering on its commitments to their stakeholders. Focus is achieved using concepts such as the Product Owner, collocation, whole team, and daily Scrums. However, this inward focus and self-reliance can lead to silo behavior whereby the team ignores enterprise concerns such as basic governance, reuse of assets, patterns, templates and guidelines. Disparate architectures and systems that are difficult to maintain can result. DAD encourages teams to be enterprise aware, and to include the Architecture Owner role, to ensure that good enterprise practices are not ignored, and that collaboration occurs between projects and enterprise authorities as required.
3. Greater practice breadth. DAD is a hybrid decision process framework that adopts strategies from a wide range of sources, including Scrum, Extreme Programming (XP), Agile Modeling, Kanban, Outside in Development (OID) and many more and shows how they fit together. Instead of focusing on a small part of the overall delivery process, as Scrum does, DAD addresses a much wider scope and as a result provides more robust and effective guidance to agile teams.
4. Less prescription. DAD promotes a goals-driven approach which enables more effective tailoring and scaling. For example, one of the DAD process goals is *Address Changing Stakeholder Needs*. Where Scrum prescribes a single way to do this, the product backlog,

DAD gives you several options (Product Backlog, Work Item List, Work Item Pool, Formal Change Management) as well as advice for when to consider each strategy. DAD also defaults to Work Item List, a more robust extension of a Product Backlog, giving you a good starting point. Another goal is *Coordinate Activities*. Where Scrum prescribes a 15-minute daily meeting called a Daily Scrum Meeting or Daily Stand Up, DAD gives you several options to choose from and walks you through how to choose the right approach for you.

5. Less branding. One of the philosophies we took when describing DAD was that we wanted to move away from the process branding that we've seen occurring in the agile community. Although DAD is flexible when it comes to terminology, for example if you want to use the term Sprint instead of Iteration then go right ahead, DAD defaults to non-branded terms. So, for example we use the terms Coordination Meeting over Scrum Meeting, Team Lead over ScrumMaster, Retrospective over Sprint Retrospective, and so on.

Scrum of Scrum

Scrum of Scrum Framework – Managing multiple scrum teams by representation for same product or project.

The Scrum of Scrums is a scaling mechanism. Scrum scales fractally and by doing so limits the number of communication pathways needed to transmit information relevant to the success of the enterprise. The Scrum of Scrums is analogous to the team level Daily Scrum except the Scrum of Scrums is a virtual team composed of representatives from several individual Scrum teams that collaborate to integrate and ship a product(s). The Scrum Masters and anyone else needed to deliver the Scrum of Scrums collaborative Definition of Done meet and communicate impediments, progress, and any cross-team coordination that needs to happen by answering for the team the same three questions used in the Daily Scrum.

A technique to scale Scrum up to large groups (over a dozen people), consisting of dividing the groups into Agile teams of 5-10. Each daily scrum within a sub-team ends by designating one member as "ambassador" to participate in a daily meeting with ambassadors from other teams, called the Scrum of Scrums.

Large Scale Scrum

LeSS is a scaled-up version of one-team Scrum, and it maintains many of the practices and ideas of one-team Scrum. In LeSS, you will find:

- a single Product Backlog (because it's for a product, not a team),
- one Definition of Done for all teams,
- one Potentially Shippable Product Increment at the end of each Sprint,
- one Product Owner,
- many complete, cross-functional teams (with no single-specialist teams),
- one Sprint.

In LeSS all Teams are in a common Sprint to deliver a common shippable product, every Sprint.

What's Different in LeSS?

- Sprint Planning Part 1: In addition to the one Product Owner, it includes people from all teams. Let team members self-manage to decide their division of Product Backlog Items. Team members also discuss opportunities to find shared work and cooperate, especially for related items.
- Sprint Planning Part 2: This is held independently (and usually in parallel) by each Team, though sometimes for simple coordination and learning two or more Teams may hold it in the same room (in different areas).
- Daily Scrum: This is also held independently by each Team, though a member of Team A may observe Team B's Daily Scrum, to increase information sharing.
- Coordination: Just Talk, Communicate in Code, Travelers, Open Space, and Communities.
- Overall PBR: There may be an optional and short overall Product Backlog Refinement (PBR) meeting that includes the one Product Owner and people from all teams. The key purpose is to decide which teams are likely to implement which items and therefore select those items for later in-depth single-team PBR. It is also a chance to increase alignment with the Product Owner and all teams.
- Product Backlog Refinement: The only requirement in LeSS is single-team PBR, the same as in one-team Scrum. But a common and useful variation is multi-team PBR, where two or more Teams are in the same room together, to increase learning and coordination.
- Sprint Review: In addition to the one Product Owner, it includes people from all teams, and relevant customers/users and other stakeholders. For the phase of inspecting the product increment and new items, consider a "bazaar" or "science fair" style: a large room with multiple areas, each staffed by team members, where the items developed by teams are shown and discussed.
- Overall Retrospective: This is a new meeting not found in one-team Scrum, and its purpose is to explore improving the overall system, rather than focusing on one Team. The maximum duration is 45 minutes per week of Sprint. It includes the Product Owner, Scrum Masters, and rotating representatives from each Team.

Nexus

Nexus Framework - Many scrum teams along with integration team.

NEXUS FRAMEWORK

Nexus is an Agile framework used in a scaled agile project when there are approximately three to nine Scrum development teams. Each team consists of five to nine members, and there is one common product backlog used by all the teams.

Many dependencies arise between the work of multiple teams. The teams collaborate to create a complete and "Done" Increment at least every Sprint. These dependencies relate to:

Requirements: The scope of the requirements may overlap, and how they are implemented may also affect each other. This should be considered while ordering the Product Backlog and selecting requirements.

Domain knowledge: The team-members know various business and computer systems. That knowledge should be mapped to the Scrum Teams to ensure its adequate. and, to minimize interruptions between teams during a Sprint.

Software and test artefacts: The requirements are or will be instantiated in software code and test suites.

Dependency between teams can be reduced up to some extent if the team's knowledge, need and code/test artefacts are mapped to the same Scrum Teams.

Integration Team

The core of the Nexus framework is the integration team which consists of a Product Owner, Scrum Master, and one or more members from each team. The purpose of the integration team is to coordinate the work of all the Scrum teams. This team make sure their completed work inter-meshes together and is in harmony and not conflict. The need for an integration team becomes even more essential the larger the number of Scrum teams. These teams, all working on the same project and using the same product backlog.

Process Flow

With Nexus, there is a standard product backlog which is refined as best as possible. The goal is to find work a given team can do on its own without dependence on other teams. At the Nexus sprint planning meeting, each team picks out from the product backlog the items they plan to work on during the next sprint. This is done in communication with the other teams. This is again done to reduce dependencies. By the meeting's end, a shared product backlog emerges and the overall Nexus goal the teams want to accomplish in the next sprint is determined. There also is an output of a single sprint backlog where all the tasks are tagged to indicate which team is responsible for what.

In a sprint, multiple integrations are done on daily basis to immediately identify and resolve coding conflicts.

To get this work properly all teams must integrate their completed product into the code base at least once daily.

Each team, like in Scrum, has a Daily Scrum meeting but besides, there is a Daily Nexus Scrum meeting (a Scrum of Scrums). Here progress is reported, along with problems, by each team's representative. The information gleaned from the meeting is then taken back by each representative to his or her team.

There also is a Nexus sprint retrospective meeting after the completion of a sprint. A discussion of what needs to change for individual teams, and what is affecting all the teams that need to change. If there are no changes to be made the wary assumption is that the project is moving along on time with 100% integration for all code written to date.

Nexus is designed to handle projects with up to 100 people. A new framework called Nexus plus is used for projects that call for over 100 people, perhaps thousands. For very large projects Nexus plus is used where there are multiple 100-person Nexus teams.

All work in a Nexus may be done by all members of the Scrum Teams, as cross-functional members of the Nexus. Based on dependencies, the teams may select the most appropriate members to do specific work.

Product Backlog Refinement:

The Product Backlog needs to be groomed so that dependencies are identified and removed. Product Backlog items are refined into thinly sliced pieces of functionality. The work team is likely to do should be identified as early as possible.

Nexus Sprint Planning:

Representatives from each Scrum Team meet to discuss and review the refined Product Backlog. They select Product Backlog items for each team. Each Scrum Team then plans its Sprint, interacting with other teams as appropriate. The outcome is a set of Sprint Goals that align with the overarching Nexus Goal, each Scrum Team's Sprint Backlog and a single Nexus Sprint Backlog. The Nexus Sprint Backlog makes the Scrum Team's selected Product Backlog items and any dependencies transparent.

Development work:

All teams frequently integrate their work into a common environment that can be tested to ensure that the integration is done.

Nexus Daily Scrum:

Representatives from each Scrum team meet daily to identify if any integration issues exist. If identified, this information is transferred back to each Scrum Team's Daily Scrum. Scrum Teams then use their Daily Scrum to create a plan for the day, being sure to address the integration issues raised during the Nexus Daily Scrum.

Nexus Sprint Review: All teams meet with the Product Owner to review the Integrated Increment. Adjustments may be made to the Product Backlog.

Nexus Sprint Retrospective: Representatives from each Scrum Team meet to identify shared challenges. Then, each Scrum Team holds individual Sprint Retrospectives. Representatives from each team meet again to discuss any actions needed based on shared challenges.

Scalable Agile Framework

SAFe is designed to help businesses efficiently deliver value on a regular and predictable schedule.

It provides a knowledge base of proven principles and practices to support enterprise agility.

It provides a simple, lightweight experience for the software development team. The whole framework is divided into three segments Team, Program and Portfolio. There is one optional segment- Large Solution.

SAFe allows team for,
- Implementing Lean-Agile software and systems in enterprise level
- It's based on Lean and Agile principles.
- It gives detailed guidance for work at the enterprise Portfolio, Value Stream, Program, and Team.
- It's designed to meet the needs of all stakeholders within an organization.

Let's see how Scaled Agile framework is different from other agile practices,
- It's publicly available and free to use.
- Available in a highly approachable and usable form.
- It's lightweight, practically proven results and specific to level.
- It constantly/regularly modifies/maintains most commonly used agile practices.
- Offers useful extensions to common agile practices.
- Grounds agile practices to an enterprise context.
- Offers complete picture of software development.
- Visibility or transparency is more on all the levels.
- Continues or regular feedback on quality and improvement.

Scaled Agile Framework (SAFe): It stands on the foundations of its
- Lean-Agile Principles
- Core Values,
- Lean-Agile Leadership
- Lean-Agile Mind-set,

SAFe Lean-Agile Principles

These basic principles and values for SAFe must be understood to get the desired results.
- Take an economic view

- Apply systems thinking
- Assume variability; preserve options
- Build incrementally with fast, integrated learning cycles
- Base milestones on an objective evaluation of working systems
- Visualize and limit WIP, reduce batch sizes and manage queue lengths
- Apply cadence, synchronize with cross-domain planning
- Unlock the intrinsic motivation of knowledge workers
- Decentralize decision-making

SAFe Agile Core Values

The SAFe agile is based on these four values.

Alignment:

- SAFe supports alignment.
- Alignment starts at,
    - Strategic Themes in Portfolio Backlog and moves down to Vision and Roadmap of Program Backlogs and then moves to the Team Backlogs.

Built-in Quality:

- It ensures that every incremental delivery reflects the quality standards.
- Quality is not "added later" is built in.
- Built-in quality is a prerequisite of Lean and its mandatory

Transparency:

- Transparency is the enabler for trust.
- SAFe helps the enterprise to achieve transparency at all levels- Executives, Portfolio Managers, and other stakeholders.
- Everyone can see into the portfolio backlog/Kanban, program backlogs/Kanban, and Team Backlog/Kanban.
- Each level has a clear understanding of the PI goals.
- Train Programs have visibility into the team's backlogs, as well other program backlogs
- Teams and programs have visibility into business and architecture Epics. They can see what might be headed their way.

Program Execution:

- SAFe places great focus on working systems and resultant business outcomes.
- SAFe is not useful if teams can't execute and continuously deliver value.

Lean Agile Leaders:

The Lean-Agile Leaders are lifelong learners and teachers. It helps teams to build better systems through understanding and exhibiting the Lean-Agile SAFe Principles.

As an enabler for the teams, the ultimate responsibility is adoption, success and ongoing improvement of Lean-Agile developments. For the change and continuous improvement, leaders must be trained.

Leaders need to adopt a new style of leadership. One that truly empowers and engages individuals and teams to reach their highest potential.

Principles of these Lean-Agile Leaders

- Lead the Change
- Know the Way; Emphasize Lifelong Learning
- Develop People
- Inspire and Align with Mission; Minimize Constraints
- Decentralize Decision-Making
- Unlock the Intrinsic Motivation of Knowledge Workers

Lean Agile Mind-Set:

Lean-Agile mindset is represented in two things:

1. The SAFe House of Lean
2. Agile Manifesto

The SAFe House of Lean:

SAFe is derived from Lean manufacturing principles and practices. Based on these factors SAFe presents the "SAFe House of Lean". It is inspired by "house" of lean Toyota.

The Goal of lean is unbeatable: To deliver maximum customer value in the shortest lead time with the highest possible quality to customer.

VISA Methodology

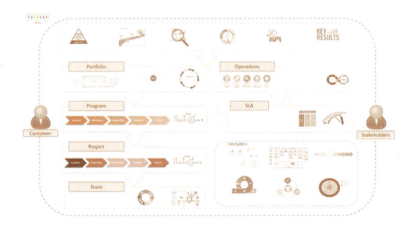

VISA Methodology for agile projects are set of standards and practices with templates and sample to help agile team to guide in following agile practices based on project requirements

PART D

Key Metrics

One of the more important metrics we look at for our own engineering team, as well as for the engineering teams using Velocity, is Cycle Time. Cycle Time is, very roughly, a measure of process speed.

Software development Team tend to ignore cycle time, perhaps because they feel that they are already getting things done as fast as they can. In fact, reducing batch sizes and addressing capacity bottlenecks can reduce cycle time quite a bit, even in organizations that consider themselves efficient already.

In other words, rather than trust your gut that you're moving as fast as possible, why not supplement your understanding with a quantitative measure? As with other metrics, tracking cycle time can reduce bias and provide a trustworthy baseline from which to drive improvement.

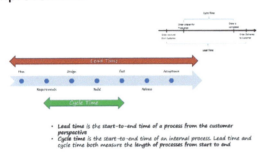

- Lead time is the start-to-end time of a process from the customer perspective
- Cycle time is the start-to-end time of an internal process. Lead time and cycle time both measure the length of processes from start to end

One of the challenges with agile methods is to get a clear perspective on how to measure process improvements.

in an *ideal* agile environment:
1. As before, the Customer / User / Stakeholder sees a need, validates it and submits a request to have that need fulfilled.
2. That request is immediately placed in a ready state for the next iteration (cycle, sprint) of a delivery team. Elapsed time: maximum one month.
3. Team completes the request including all work to deliver/deploy and work is delivered to the stakeholder at the end of the iteration. Elapsed time: maximum two months.

So, the ideal method of doing agile has a maximum cycle time of two months to deliver from the time a request is made... how many teams are doing this? Not many.

Depending on the type of request, the cycle time for a piece of work can vary widely. Some low priority items may take years even in an agile environment. A low priority request is made and approved but then never quite makes it into a project... and then once in a project never quite makes it to the top of the team's product backlog.

The predominant factor in most organizations' cycle time is the number and size of the queues they use as work is processed. In most organizations there are several queues and most of them contain large numbers of requests or bits of work in process. Queues represent huge amounts of waste. It is easy to see that queue size and cycle time are closely related: the more items in a queue, the longer the cycle time.

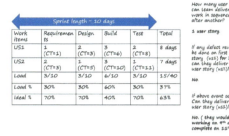

How many user stories can team deliver if they work in sequences one after another?

1 user story.

If any defect rework to be done on first user story (US1) for 3 days, can they deliver second user story (US2)?

No.

If above event occurs, Can they deliver first user story (US1)?

No. (they would start working on 9th day and complete on 11th day)

Efficiency

The percentage of tasks delivered as per specific guidelines. While customer-centricity emphasizes on building the right product at the right time for the right market, knowing how much your teams were able to accomplish successfully against the list of planned tasks gets you accurate insights on both your current resources and their capabilities. Moreover, it gives you an overview of the complexities, casting a shadow over tasks in terms of time, scope and budgeting constraints, thus helping you identify the ones that overran original estimates.

Teams get clarification on their work packages. The measure itemizes the number of stories committed to in the sprint planning and assesses how many of them are marked as completed.

Your staff can then divide their focus on different aspects of the same user story and work on it in parallel rather than in sequential blocks. For example, if you're building a flight ticketing system, the development team can create user stories capturing bookings, cancellations, refunds, date changes and points-based mileage. Each member can estimate their efforts by profiling the project on those aspects that are easy to recreate by simply rewriting code where applicable.

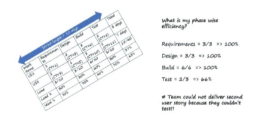

What is my phase wise efficiency?

Requirements = 3/3 => 100%

Design = 3/3 => 100%

Build = 6/6 => 100%

Test = 2/3 => 66%

Team could not deliver second user story because they couldn't test!!

At time due to prioritization glitches and reduced focus, below situation might occur leading to non-delivery of any shippable product out of sprint even though your efficiency is at expectable level. Beware of such situation.

Never compromise on flow or cycle time requirements, Team can work in parallel, however they work must be flow units rather than functional units, it is possible few team members priority would result in working on work items that might not help in assembling or integrating to ship them out and causing deadlock and increasing lead time or delivery time of product readiness to customer.

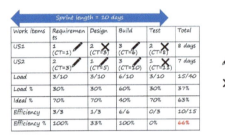

Work items	Requirements	Design	Build	Test	Total
US1	1 (CT=1)	2 (CT=3)	3 (CT=6)	2 (CT=8)	8 days
US2	2 (CT=3)	1 (CT=5)	3 (CT=10)	1 (CT=11)	7 days
Load	3/10	3/10	6/10	3/10	15/40
Load %	30%	30%	60%	30%	37%
Ideal %	70%	70%	40%	70%	63%
Efficiency	3/3	1/3	6/6	0/3	10/15
Efficiency %	100%	33%	100%	0%	66%

Productivity & Throughput: Improving cycle time can now be done in a few ways:
1. Put a cap on the number of items in the work queue. Since cycle time is directly related to the size of the queues in a system, this is a sure way of putting a maximum on cycle time.
2. Go through all existing requests and throw as many away as possible. This can be tough to do, but if you are able to do a cost benefit analysis, you will typically find that older items in the queue are no longer worthwhile.
3. Provide more stringent gating functions for allowing requests onto the queue. The few items added, the faster the size of the queue is reduced.
4. And of course, increase the performance of your team(s) so that they go through items on the queue more quickly.

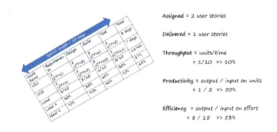

Assigned = 2 user stories

Delivered = 1 user stories

Throughput = units/time
= 1/10 => 10%

Productivity = output / input on units
= 1 / 2 => 50%

Efficiency = output / input on effort
= 8 / 15 => 53%

ROI is in its simplest form a measure of how much benefit there is to do something as compared to the cost of doing it. It considers the importance of time and timing, the importance of other options you may have, and business reality of your work. It also considers costs.

In software development, the primary cost is the cost of the staff doing the work, and the time factor is your cycle time. If you have a consistent team working on iterations that are always the same size and if you have little or no work being done outside of the iterations, it is very easy to calculate ROI in a useful way. Simply measure how much value a given iteration worth of work will generate and divide by the cost of the team for an iteration (and if the team is not yet doing work as it considers the time value of money since the work might not be done for several iterations). Now, productivity is simply a measure of the Return for each Team-Iteration. Dollars/iteration.

If the team's productivity goes down, you can ask some simple questions:
- Did the expected return of the work go down? If so, is there more valuable work the team should be doing? This becomes an opportunity for product improvement.
- If not, what caused the team to get less done? Was the work harder than expected? Was there a skill gap? Was there an organizational obstacle that was revealed? Was someone sick? This becomes an opportunity for process and team improvement.

Customer satisfaction can be measured in many ways. If you have already started using agile practices, there is a good chance that your customers will already be more satisfied than they were before. This will show up informally through word-of-mouth. However, it is good to have a more systematic way of measuring customer satisfaction.

Culture

The adoption of agile development continues to increase. Ninety-four percent of all organizations surveyed, the percentage of respondents with distributed agile teams jumped from 35 percent to 80 percent from 2012 to 2014. Despite the high adoption, however, many organizations struggle with high agile project failure rates.

Lack of experience with agile methods (45%)
Company philosophy or culture at odds with core agile values (40%)
Lack of management support (40%)
 External pressure to follow traditional waterfall processes (34%)
Lack of support for cultural transition (39%)
A broader organizational or communications problem (33%)
Unwillingness of team to follow agile (33%)
Insufficient training (30%)

The agile approach can be difficult to embrace not only in a culture that depends heavily on legacy systems and processes, but also in a culture that is driven by control. Agile development requires empowerment. It works only if you empower your development teams to work collaboratively and entrepreneurially. This is one of the reasons why top-down cultural adoption is critical to corporate agile transformation success.

Overall, an organization's culture is the product of its tools, processes and control mechanisms. Therefore, to successfully change its culture, an organization needs to change, among other things, its tools, processes and control mechanisms. Despite these barriers, agile development drives value for any type of organization and should be considered—not as a silver bullet for all delivery solutions—but in situations where it makes business sense. Digitalization, customer onboarding solutions or any initiative requiring a faster response to changing customer expectations are strong candidates for agile delivery.

How do large, complex organizations successfully transition to agile? How do they change their culture? How do they overcome past agile failures and ensure future agile successes? Below are key success factors for building an agile culture,

Business and IT leadership engagement Agile projects and programs will not survive in large hierarchical organizations that have traditional command and control cultures without C-level support—period. The decision and drive to change how the organization operates must come from the top down. It also must involve both business and technology operations, as most operational areas need to change for Agile to take root. IT can't implement agile alone. A close relationship and close collaboration between business and IT leadership is crucial. Enterprise agile must be co-owned.

Organizational readiness Most organizations cannot go "all agile" at once. Instead, they need a transitional roadmap that provides the right amount of support based on the organization's readiness. A purist approach to agile—where traditional development is completely replaced in one fell swoop—results in failure for many organizations, especially those that rely on tight controls, rigid structures and cost-benefit analysis. To build an effective change strategy, you must understand where the organization is at and define transitional phases in line with its maturity and readiness.

Team empowerment in addition, agile requires strong team empowerment. IT teams must work differently when implementing agile. In a traditional waterfall environment, teams align themselves to a specific function such as development or testing, relying on processes and templates, and without a big picture view. They also often work in silos. Agile requires flexibility and close collaboration with teams who align to focus on the successful outcome of the initiative, regardless of function. Agile also provides teams with a great deal of transparency into the business objectives behind their work. Working this way requires top-to-bottom change management that leads to a "learn and change" culture. In this kind of a culture, teams are empowered to innovate and create based on an understanding of where the business is headed and with the autonomy to act independently and collaboratively. We repeatedly see pockets of middle management actively or covertly pushing back on the agile transformation. This is understandable because, when we empower the worker, we don't need as many layers of management. Swift, firm action from executives is required to address pushback from non-conformers. The organization needs to know that agile transformation is here to stay.

Transitional transformation Building the right transitional plan to agile requires bringing together people, processes and technologies and identifying where it makes business sense to implement agile. As we noted above, agile is not a silver bullet. An assessment of the areas where agile would work best is required, which will then guide the transition. Many organizations start doing agile iterations right away, which can be too difficult. A well-defined transitional approach is required.

Transitioning to agile can't be done in an agile way for many organizations. An effective program for managing the transition and driving cultural change is required. Three key program requirements include the following:

• Communication: This is the most critical requirement. Clear and consistent communication between the business and IT sides and among IT teams creates the level of engagement, understanding and collaboration required for agile success.

 • Buy-in from the top down: A bottom up approach to agile adoption needs to be supported from the top to be successful. Buy-in needs to cascade from the top down.

• Ongoing business and IT collaboration: As discussed previously, IT cannot implement agile alone. Business leadership needs to be involved from the outset and remained involved, providing ongoing input into business direction and objectives to guide the agile development.

PART E

GAMES

To win game, the team needs agility. The games can be group based on domain and lifecycle frameworks.

Olympics individual games are better suitable for Domain Frameworks

Olympics Team games are better suitable for lifecycle frameworks.

Agile VISA Methodology is not framework, rather methodology describing steps and actions to be performed during project execution and delivery.

The best games suitable for Methodology is one of marital arts formats – preferable Bo-Staff.

Origami

Origami from ori meaning "folding", and kami meaning "paper" (kami changes to gami due to rendaku)) is the art of paper folding, which is often associated with Japanese culture. In modern usage, the word "origami" is used as an inclusive term for all folding practices, regardless of their culture of origin. The goal is to transform a flat square sheet of paper into a finished sculpture through folding and sculpting techniques. Modern origami practitioners generally discourage the use of cuts, glue, or markings on the paper. Origami folders often use the Japanese word kirigami to refer to designs which use cuts, although cutting is more characteristic of Chinese papercrafts. [failed verification]

The small number of basic origami folds can be combined in a variety of ways to make intricate designs. The best-known origami model is the Japanese paper crane. In general, these designs begin with a square sheet of paper whose sides may be of different colors, prints, or patterns. Traditional Japanese origami, which has been practiced since the Edo period (1603–1867), has often been less strict about these conventions, sometimes cutting the paper or using no square shapes to start with. The principles of origami are also used in stents, packaging and other engineering applications.

Purpose: This game helps in identifying right domain framework for agile project phases.

Brain Games - ART

The ART – Brain game is modeling practice to identify the current practices and process.

To start with game, the team needs to collect the current way of practices and process being practiced and model it.

Once model is created, the team discuss together to identify alterative models applying SWOT techniques and RCA methods to recommend best process.

This game helps in innovation from current practices as well as knowing existing system better.

Purpose: To bring innovation in practice within team.

Game of Business

Business game (also called business simulation game) refers to simulation games that are used as an educational tool for teaching business. Business games may be carried out for various business training such as: general management, finance, organizational behaviour, human resources, etc. Often, the term "business simulation" is used with the same meaning.

A business game has been defined as "a game with a business environment that can lead to one or both of the following results: the training of players in business skills (hard and/or soft) or the evaluation of players' performances (quantitatively and/or qualitatively)".[1]

Business games are used as a teaching method in universities, and more particularly in business schools, but also for executive education.

Purpose: This game helps in identifying right team process framework based on context of business.

Target Board

Basic Target Gameplay

Target shuffleboard is played the same way as regular shuffleboard, except there is a target area for the scoring instead of foul lines. This version can also be played by individuals or in teams. Briefly, the objective is to slide all four of your pucks against those of your opponent, so that they reach the highest scoring area without falling off the end of the board. Players take turns sliding their pucks until all eight pucks have been slid. This completes the turn and only the winner scores. The game is usually played until 21 points, but that can vary.

How to Throw the Shuffleboard Pucks In Target

Players typically decide by coin toss who shall shoot first and which colour each shall have. Standing at the same end of the table, the first player shuffles the first puck toward the Target at the opposite end of the playing field. The opponent then shuffles their first puck, attempting either to knock off the other player's puck or to place their own in a higher scoring position. At the end of each round, the player, or team, whose puck is in the highest scoring zone is winner of that round. The players then proceed to the opposite end of the shuffleboard, and another frame is begun, with the winner of the previous frame shooting first puck.

How to Score Shuffleboard in Target

The player's score per frame is determined by adding the values of all their leading pucks that lie in a higher scoring position than an opponent's highest scoring weight. The value of the winner's scoring pucks is determined by the Target zone in which they lie.

Any puck on the board that clears the foul line nearest the players and does not completely clear the line of the outer or larger Target ring scores one-point. Pucks that completely clear the outer Target ring and lie within larger ring zone or that don't completely clear the line of the intermediate ring score two-points. Any pucks that completely clear the line of the intermediate ring and lie within the zone between it and the black inner ring score three-points. A puck that in any way touches the black inner ring of the target scores four-points, whereas a puck that completely covers the black inner ring of the target scores five-points.

Purpose: This game helps team to focus towards project goals. The team must first identify project purpose and its dependencies. Once done, they need to focus on Goal and try to hit on board at random and analyse impact to goal.

Math + Art

In the *Math Art and Drawing Games for Kids book,* you'll find an amazing collection of more than 40 hands-on art activities that make learning about math fun!

- Make pixel art using graph paper, grids, and dot grids.
- Explore projects that teach symmetry with mandala drawings, stained glass rose window art, and more.
- Use equations, counting, addition, and multiplication to create Fibonacci and golden rectangle art.
- Play with geometric shapes like spirals, hexagrams, and tetrahedrons.
- Learn about patterns and motifs used by cultures from all over the world, including Native American porcupine quill art, African Kente prints, and labyrinths from ancient Crete.
- Create fine art-inspired projects using math, including Escher's tessellations, Kandinski's abstractions, and Alexander Calder's mobiles.
- Cook up some delicious math by making cookie tangrams, waffle fractions, and bread art.

Purpose: This game helps in identifying the right frameworks based on project nature.

Creative Art Let's Innovate

Refers to participation in a range of activities that allow for creative and imaginative expression, such as music, art, creative movement, and drama.

The creative arts engage children's minds, bodies, and senses. The arts invite children to listen, observe, discuss, move, solve problems, and imagine using multiple modes of thought and self-expression.

The creative arts provide ways for professionals and learners to learn and use skills in other domains.

In the domain of Creative Arts Expression, programs need to ensure that children who are dual language learners can demonstrate their abilities, skills, and knowledge in any language, including their home language

Purpose: This game helps the team to apply process and practices of VISA methodology for agile projects.

Appendixes

- Bibliography
- Glossary
- Books to Read

Bibliography

References:

https://info.convedo.com/the-6-building-blocks-for-agile-transformation

https://en.wikipedia.org/wiki/PDCA

https://www.visual-paradigm.com/guide/uml-unified-modeling-language/what-is-uml/#composite-structure-diagram

https://www.agilealliance.org

https://existek.com/blog/sdlc-models/

https://www.allaboutlean.com/pdca-history/

https://www.project-management-prepcast.com/free/pmi-acp-exam/articles/844-traditional-vs-agile-project-management-common-concepts-with-different-implementations

https://www.youtube.com/playlist?list=PLs8F9-fy20QQ3UcgiFCcoyhXn5T0bq_3G

https://techbeacon.com/app-dev-testing/4-biggest-challenges-moving-scaled-agile-framework-safe

https://techbeacon.com/app-dev-testing/cracking-safe-experts-take-scaled-agile-framework

Glossary

Term	Meaning
Architecture	Representation of Framework or connected process and methods (what?)
ASD	Adaptive Software Development Framework
Backlogs	Collection of items to work upon.
Burndowns	Amount of work completed and remaining against time allotted.
Cycle Time	Cycle time is the start-to-end time of an internal process. Lead time and cycle time both measure the length of processes from start to end
DAD	Distributed Agile Delivery Framework
Decomposition	Breaking bigger into smaller pieces. Requirements are usually decomposed to smaller requirements.
DevOps	Software development and support operations practices by applying common methods.
DSDM	Dynamic System Development Methods Framework
Effectiveness	Delivering right work as expected by customer (quality - meeting requirements)
Efficiency	The ratio of work delivered against work allocated [output/input on effort]
FDD	Feature Driven Development Methods

Framework	Set of process and methods focused to provide solution (not solve) - (What?)
Generalization	Grouping or classification of requirements or class. Used to understand commonalities and helps in modelling inheritance.
IID	Iterative and Incremental Development focus in Iterative design and incremental builds or developments.
Incremental	Action of performing work in partial or in pieces.
Iteration	It is also called sprint with fixed length of time to complete work or functionality.
Iterative	Action of performing work over and over (repeatedly) until it is accepted.
Kanban	Lean method to improve bottlenecks and balancing demands with capacity.
Lead Time	Lead time is the start-to-end time of a process from the customer perspective
Lean SD	Lean Software Development is framework applying lean principles and practices (applying methods).
MDE	Model driven engineering
Method	Set of steps to followed fix problem – It's a solution to problem. (How?)
Methodology	Applying tools and methods against process to obtain expected solution to given problem or scenarios (How?)
Mockup	Production look of page or screen for user.

Model	Representation of process, methods, framework, Standalone or Connected.
Procedure	Set of methods to follow to solve given problem – it's a solution to problem (How?)
Process	Action to convert input to desired output. (What?)
Productivity	The rate or speed at which workable product is produced in connected process or system with quality [output/input on units]
RAD	Rapid Application Development - it uses adaptive concepts and methods.
SAFe	Scalable Agile framework focused in managing large teams (Scale) along with LeSS, DAD and Nexus.
Sprint	It is also called iteration with fixed length of time to complete functionality or backlogs items
Story board	User actions in system represented in form of visuals (wireframes with user actions against scenarios)
Story points	Measure of user story complexity by applying Fibonacci series.
Throughput	The rate or speed at which workable product is produced in connected process or system over time [units/time].
Timeboxing	Fixed period allocated called as Timebox to set of functionalities.
Trend	Over a period. (velocity trend, defects trend, etc.)
UP	Unified software development Process - framework adopting iterative and incremental process.

Velocity	The rate at which work items are delivered by team [units/time]
WBS	Tabular timetable that includes project tasks grouped by project phases and organized into work packages to identify the amount of work the project team is expected to perform, and to specify the period available for the team to do their project tasks.
Wireframe	A rough sketch or visual of what page or screen looks like for user.
Workflow	Connected business process (what) where tasks, information or documents are passed from one participant to another for action, according to a set of procedural rules. (how?)
XP	Extreme Programming is methodology focused in meeting changing customer needs by adopting short cycle times.

Books to Read

- Agile Estimating and Planning, Mike Cohn, 2005
- Essential Scrum: A Practical Guide to the Most Popular Agile Process, Kenneth S. Rubin, 2012
- The Agile Samurai: How Agile Masters Deliver Great Software, Jonathan Rasmusson, 2010
- Agile Project Management, Jim Highsmith, 2004
- User Stories Applied, Mike Cohn, 2004
- More Agile Testing: Learning Journeys for the Whole Team, Lisa Crispin, 2015
- Collaboration Explained: Facilitation Skills for Software Project Leaders, Jean Tabaka, 2006
- Getting Value Out of Agile Retrospectives - A Toolbox of Retrospective Exercises, Ben Linders and Luis Gonçalves, 2014
- Agile Software Requirements: Lean Requirements Practices for Teams, Programs, and the Enterprise, Dean Leffingwell, 2010
- The Project Manager's Guide to Mastering Agile: Principles and Practices for an Adaptive Approach, Charles G. Cobb, 2015

Quick Reference (Table View)

Plan	Requirements	Estimation	Design	Build	Test	Support
Backlogs	Definition of Done.	Poker card	Design Thinking	Incremental	Test Early	Continuous deployment
Refinement	Progressive Elaboration	3-Point	Get Creative	Unit Test	Verify and Validate	
Sprints	Delivery Mapping	UCP	Continioues	Continuous integration	Defect prevention	
Retrospective	Track as Whole	Delphi	Iterative development	Mockup	Quality assurance	
Velocity	Prioritized lists	T-Size	Brainstorming	Prototype	Quality control	
Burndown	Decomposition		Modelling		Defect Triage	
Audit	Requirements Classification				Defect Prioritization	
Inspection	Requirements Grouping				Defect Classification	
Budget	Grooming				Pareto	
Rolling Wave	Requirements Complexity				Sanity Testing	
Grooming	Elaboration and Sizing				Functional Testing	
	Wireframe				Regression Testing	
	User story				Performance Testing	
	Features				Accessibility Testing	
	Epics or Themes				Security Testing	
	Story board				Load Testing	
	Personas				Smoke Testing	
					Defect Resolution	

Quick Reference (Description)

Definition of Done: A checklist of the types of work that the team is expected to complete within the iteration.
Backlog: A list of work items (mostly prioritized, time to time)

Poker card: Cards being used for sizing the product backlog items.

Refinement/Grooming: An activity of refining the backlog items.

Sprint: Timeboxed iterations usually one to four weeks.

Retrospective: An activity of inspect and adapt. This is the last activity of every iteration.

Velocity: An amount of work done in each iteration.

Burndown Chart: A chart representing remaining amount of work.

Continuous integration: A technical practice where teams integrate their work as frequently as possible.

Continuous deployment: A practice of deploying each new feature to users soon after building and testing.
Iterative development: Incremental development incorporating feedback loops.

T Shirt-Size: A technic of relative size estimation (S, L, XL, XXL, etc.)

Epics: A very large piece of functionality which generally serves the purpose of place holder. Epic can further be broken in to features and user stories.

Features: A piece of functionality that is meaningful to a user. This can further be broken in to user stories.

User story: A user story describes functionality that will be valuable to a user. It is a small business
objective understandable for both business people and technical people. They are structured in a format such as "As a <user role> I want to achieve <goal> so that I get <benefit>."

 3-Point: It is estimation technique based on least, average and maximum time an activity could be performed. The average of 3 factors are considered in determining the efforts.

UCP – Use case Points – This estimation technique evolved post OOPS became default standard, this technique focuses on Technical, environmental and complexity of each user interaction in system to determine effort.

Delphi – The estimation technique averages based on experience of experts in team to determine effort.
Story board – Story board is also termed as Kanban board standing for meaning view board. It is used to represent current state of work items in identified flow for working team.

Personas – It is representing application users or actors interacting with system to fulfill their objectives.

Progressive elaboration involves continuously improving and detailing a plan as more detailed and specific information and more accurate estimates become available.

Elicitation: requirements elicitation is the practice of researching and discovering the requirements of a system from users, customers, and other stakeholders. The practice is also sometimes referred to as "requirement gathering".

Delivery Mapping – An approach to map user stories to delivery plan promoting shippable and workable components.

Track as Whole – It represent base unit in agile team to deliver components at end of each sprint, usually in forms of user journeys or system flows or epics.

Prioritized list – It is list of backlog work items where priority is set for team to work upon.

Decomposition – It is methods of breaking complex units to smaller manageable units.

Requirements Classification – It is practice determining between functional vs non-functional requirements.
Requirements Grouping – set of requirements related to each other are grouped to common domain and are often termed as features or functionality of application.

Requirements Complexity – It is method to determine complexity level to develop based on expected activity to perform. High, Medium, Small are more commonly used complexity terms and are generally mapped to story points.

Elaboration and Sizing - A method to determine effort required to implement requirement based on time required for set of related activity to perform to complete.

Wireframe – It is basic visual representation of application screen to user detailing on information to capture or show or possible actions to perform.
Mockup: A model of a program or structure, used for experimental purposes.